TENNIS
for the Bloody Fun of It

TENNIS
for the Bloody Fun of It

ROD LAVER *and* ROY EMERSON
with Barry Tarshis

Quadrangle | The New York Times Book Co.

Library of Congress Catalog Card Number: 75-11479

International Standard Book Number: 0-8129-0590-3

Book design: Tere Lo Prete

CONTENTS

INTRODUCTION
by Barry Tarshis

When word first got out about two years ago that Rod Laver and Roy Emerson were conducting tennis camps for adults, a lot of people were suspicious. And not without good reason. It was the practice among many resorts at the time—and still is, to some extent—to hire "name" players as window dressing. Then to plaster their brochures and magazine ads with photographs of the tennis star, never mind that he or she is actually there as often as Colonel Sanders visits each Kentucky Fried Chicken outlet. And even if Laver and Emerson were exceptions, there was still a question of whether players of their stature could possibly relate to and identify with the average hacker. No matter how you looked at it, it didn't smell right.

The reason I mention this is that I happened to be as skeptical as anybody about this whole business—so much so that in the latter part of 1973, I published an article in *Tennis* magazine berating the bandying of name players in the tennis resort field. The article prompted an indignant response from the vice-president of Laver-Emerson Tennis Holidays, Mike Narracott, who was upset by the fact that I hadn't singled out his company as an exception. "Come to one of our camps and see for yourself," he challenged me. "You'll be surprised."

Well, I accepted the challenge, and I *was* surprised. In December of 1973, passing through Texas on a magazine assignment, I paid a visit to a resort-development called April Sound, there to get a personal look at the Laver-Emerson Tennis Holiday operation in action. It was a revelation. Not only was Roy Emerson himself supervising and taking an active role in all six hours of the daily instruction, he was doing a bang-up job of connecting with the campers. What's more, he seemed to be having the time of his life in the process, and his exuberance had a sunny effect on everybody—even struggling beginners. Where were you, Roy Emerson, I couldn't help but wonder, when I started playing tennis.

It would be a nice touch to say here that the idea for *Tennis for the Bloody Fun of It* originated in a mystical moment when Roy was working on my backhand, but it didn't happen that way. Not exactly, anyway.

What happened was, I wrote an article—part factual, part fantasy—for *Tennis* magazine describing how it felt to be a hacker receiving instruction from a two-time Wimbledon winner. Roy liked the article. So did Rod. And so did Mike Narracott, whom I first met at a press conference in New York that summer. It was at that press conference, in fact, that I mentioned to Mike my feeling that the Laver-Emerson approach to learning tennis, exemplified by what I had seen at April Sound, would make a great book. Narracott's response was brief and to the point. "Let's do it."

So much for beginnings. When all the details of the contract had been finalized between all the participants in the book and the publisher, Quadrangle, the one thing we all agreed upon—particularly our editor at Quadrangle, Jon Segal—was that we didn't want to produce "just another tennis book." Heaven knows, there is no lack of tennis-instruction books on the market today. There are books that tell you how to play tennis, how to play better tennis, how to play better than better at tennis, how to beat your grandmother at tennis, how to achieve nirvana at tennis, ad infinitum. Remarkably, though, few if any of these books has much to say about the sheer bloody fun of it, which is what everybody connected with Rod Laver and Roy Emerson today considers the most important aspect of the game.

So that became our theme: fun. Our goal was to introduce tennis in a way that celebrated the joy of the game and to avoid the bloodless tone that creeps into so many tennis-instruction books—a tone that usually makes learning a backhand as mechanical as, say, installing a screen door.

It wasn't an easy task. More than simply presenting a technique for learning tennis, we were aiming, above all, for an attitude. This meant that simply getting 12 hours of Rod and Roy on tape wouldn't do the job. Indeed, much of the material in this book came not so much from the scheduled tape sessions as from conversations and situations that took place far from the tennis court. It's hard to estimate the exact amount of time I spent with each man. There was a week at Pinehurst, when Rod was heading up the instructional program, and a week in Houston, with Roy. There was an afternoon in Philadelphia, during the U.S. Indoor Championships. There were a couple of days in Las Vegas—disappointing in light of Rod's loss to Jimmy Connors. There were a happier three days not long after in Hartford, where Rod and Roy were part of the victorious Australian team in the Aetna World Cup. There were a number of lengthy phone conversations. And there was a final weekend in Palmetto Dunes, South Carolina, to which the Laver-Emerson organization had invited all the players who'd won tournaments at the individual Tennis Holidays.

When tennis-playing friends heard what I was up to, there was a predictable amount of ribbing, the gist of which was that with *my* tennis game, I should be paying, not receiving, money for this sort of assignment. My

reaction, usually, was to remind whoever was doing the ribbing that there was a lot more than met the eye in an assignment like this. Deep down, though, I knew I wasn't telling the truth. The fact is, it was great fun researching the book, and mainly because Rod and Roy were delightful to work with. Other writers I know who have worked with athletes on books of this nature have sour memories of the collaboration. With me, it's just the opposite. I can't remember enjoying an assignment more.

Looking back over the past nine months, I can recall with pleasure any number of conversations and situations, but none more so than the second day of the Palmetto Dunes weekend. It was a very hot day in June, and Rod and Roy, apart from working on an instructional film for most of the morning, had put in a punishing day of exhibitions and teaching. At about four in the afternoon, when the official part of the day was pretty much over, Rod and Mary invited me over to their villa for a beer. It was a typical Laver invitation. "Come over whenever you feel like. If we're not there, the door will be open. Come in and get yourself a beer. We'll be by soon."

By five that afternoon, about ten of us, mostly nontennis friends of the Lavers, were sitting around the small pool outside the villa when somebody—I don't remember who—suggested a game of volleyball in the water. Everybody knows, of course, that it's next to impossible to play a volleyball game in the water, especially when there is no net. But Rod was tickled by the idea. Within five minutes, he had constructed a makeshift net by rigging up one of those long poles you often see at private pools across the pool, supporting it—tenuously, to be sure—on two beach chairs. Then we were in the water (some of us over our heads) trying to come up with some workable rules. Again, it was all Rod. After several abortive attempts to get a reasonable game going, he quickly devised three or four rules that took into account the logistical difficulties we were playing under.

And the remarkable thing was that we managed somehow to set up a little contest that was not only a lot of fun but reasonably interesting from a competitive point of view as well—all thanks to Laver. In that short space of time, he made me realize what he meant when he once said, "You can have a hell of a good time at something and still be serious about it." Well, serious or not, by the time the team that Laver was on had shifted to the low-water side—and this was their chance to come from behind—Rod, having created the game, was giving a swimming lesson to Mike Narracott's three-year-old daughter. The volleyball game no longer commanded his interest.

About an hour later, Roy Emerson arrived, looking as if he had just hiked across the Gobi Desert. Earlier that afternoon, we were supposed to have gone over certain sections of the manuscript, but Roy politely begged off. He'd been up since seven that morning (having gone to bed well after three). He had spent the morning with Rod working on an instructional film. That afternoon, with the temperature in the mid-90s, he had conducted two clinics and played three exhibition matches. At three-thirty, when we met to talk over the manuscript, he was so tired, he said, he could barely keep his eyes open and all he wanted to do was go back to his room and take a nap. He never made it. As he was walking out of the pro shop, one of the participants in the tournament collared him and reminded him of a promise he'd made the day before at lunch, that he would work with her serve for a while. Within a half hour, there were half a dozen or so people clustered around him at one of the courts. Emmo was giving another clinic.

It was nearly six-thirty when he finally showed up at the Laver villa in the middle of an informal frisbee game. Tired as he may have been, he joined in. Then somebody—I think it was Mary Laver—thought it might be appropriate to throw Roy, still in tennis clothes, into the pool. My own feeling, when I heard the idea being discussed, was that if I were as tired as Roy Emerson looked the last thing in the world I would want was to be thrown into a swimming pool.

No matter. In Emmo went with a thunder-ous splash. Close by him in the water were three or four young kids, squealing with delight. Roy stood up slowly. He wasn't smiling and he wasn't scowling. Shaking the water from his hair, he reached into his pocket, pulled out his watch, his dripping wallet, some keys, and some change. He laid them all on the side of the pool. He still hadn't changed his expression. For a second, I wondered if he was going to leap from the water and personally manhandle everyone who had done the deed, and when a look of absolute fury suddenly crossed his face, I was convinced that this is what he was going to do.

But no. The angry look and the ear-shattering bellow that erupted from Emmo's lips were nothing more than the beginning of a make-believe sea-monster game that he proceeded to play with the kids in the water for the next half hour. To this day, I can't imagine what anybody might do, short of pouring sugar in his beer, that could make Roy Emerson angry.

Happily, I think the spirit of that afternoon is evident throughout *Tennis for the Bloody Fun of It*. We have tried to be informative in this book, but we have tried harder to make it fun. There are no gimmicks in the book— just a lot of good, solid advice for players at every level on how to play the game better and how to enjoy it more in the process. No two players in the game today, to my mind, are more qualified to talk about tennis in this regard. For if there is one thing I'll always remember about each of the weeks I spent with Rod and Roy at a Laver-Emerson Tennis Holiday it is the number of people I met who went home on the final day feeling much better about themselves than when they arrived. Tennis is one sport that gives people this opportunity. Hopefully, *Tennis for the Bloody Fun of It* will make it all the more possible.

It goes without saying that a lot of people, apart from Rod and Roy, had a hand in putting this book together. Mike Narracott, for instance, played a crucial role in coordinating the project. Kurt Markus, the Laver-Emerson Tennis Holiday's publicity director, took many of the photographs that appear throughout the book and was helpful and supportive throughout the project. All of the pros who work for the Laver-Emerson organization deserve a special thank you, and so, in particular, does Larry Jestice, who is Laver-Emerson's National Director of Tennis. Larry's only shortcoming in life, as far as I know, has been his failure to solidify my backhand. (Larry has also failed to climb Mt. Everest and I put both failures in the same category!) Ed Vebell took most of the sequence photographs. Fred Stolle contributed several "Emmo stories," despite the fact that when we first met, I mistook him for Neale Fraser, the coach of the Australian Davis Cup team. ("Neale Fraser!" Stolle replied without malice. "Hell, my backhand is much better than his.") Ginny Murrican showed flashes of genius in transforming much of the largely indecipherable mass of manuscript material into finished form. Carol Isen printed up many of the photographs. And Jon Segal's vigilant editing kept us all on our toes. Other people who either directly or indirectly made contributions to this project include Shep Campbell, the editor of *Tennis;* Stanley Braverman, the art director of *Tennis;* Laura Duggan, his assistant; Howard Brafman, a fellow "camper" at Pinehurst; Eric Hauben, Julian Padowicz, Ed Nass, Milton Kirkpatrick, Allan Isen, Les Becker, and Ed Friedlander, all of whom are gentlemanly enough when we play tennis to overlook the disparity between the level of instruction I've received and the caliber of my play. Finally, I'd like to thank my wife, Karen, whose willingness to overlook a lot of things is one of the reasons our marriage, I am happy to say, is a lot more solid than my backhand.

TENNIS
for the Bloody Fun of It

CHAPTER
1

Getting Started

Here is the situation. *You have decided to become a tennis player and you are on a tennis court for the first time. You've done your homework. You're wearing the right clothes. You own an expensive racket. You've mastered the basic lingo. You even know how to affect a knowledgeable expression as you unzip the racket cover. As if you've been doing it all your life.*

But now that you're on the court, the charade has suddenly crumbled. You never realized that a tennis court was so big, or that the net was so high. You never thought a tennis racket was so heavy or that the ball was so small. Your initial efforts are not notably successful. You take an heroic cut at the ball, and it bounces lamely into the net. You ease up on your swing, and the ball soars over the fence like a skyrocket.

You're mortified. Why didn't anybody warn you that tennis isn't nearly as easy as it looks! This spectacle you're making of yourself might not be so terrible if you were cloistered somewhere in a private court, but there you are on public display: a klutzy goldfish in tennis sneakers.

You try to cope. You shrug off your embarrassment with professional nonchalance, like a trapeze artist climbing out of his safety net. Bystanders admire your grit and spirit. Still, there is a voice deep down that wants to know why you are making a fool of yourself. You wonder: Does being a beginner have to be this painful?

Rod. I know the feeling well. Everybody who plays tennis knows the feeling. We've all been beginners ourselves. You feel as though every part of your body wants to go a different way. Nothing you do comes out right. You take what you think is a good stroke, and there goes the ball, soaring over the fence or squibbling off the side of the court.

Roy. I know the feeling, too. In fact, I still get it every now and then—especially if I'm playing Rocket Laver on one of those days when he's pulling winners out of his bloody hide.

Rod. Emmo's memory must be longer than mine, because I seem to be having less and less of those days as the years go by. Still the question here is how long a beginner has to suffer through this uncomfortable feeling we're talking about.

Roy. I'd say not long at all. Providing, that is, that you go into the game with the right atti-

tude, and that you accept the fact, above all, that you're not going to become a tennis player overnight. Nobody does. You can't expect to take a couple of lessons, play a few sets, and then call yourself a tennis player. Tennis isn't as hard to play as people make it out to be, but it's not an easy game. You have to respect the difficulties of the game if you want to start to enjoy yourself from the start.

Rod. I'll go along with that. But let's not forget that part of the fun of the game is overcoming these difficulties. Getting better. Seeing improvement in yourself. You're muddling along one day, having your usual difficulties, and then suddenly you hit a couple of great shots. They *feel* good. They sound good. It's one of the great things about tennis —the fact that just a couple of good shots can make you forget all the lousy shots.

Roy. In a way, it's even easier for a beginner to get a bang out of the game than it is for somebody who's been at it for years. What

does hitting a great backhand mean to our friend "Muscles" Rosewall? He probably gets more excited when he changes razor blades. When you've been struggling for the backhand for a couple of weeks or so, though, and you suddenly uncork a beautiful, picture backhand—well, that's something to declare a national holiday over.

Rod. But you can't really enjoy yourself as a beginner until you first get rid of all those feelings of self-consciousness that so many beginners seem to carry around with them. So what if you look a little ungainly on the court? Who cares?

Roy. Nobody, really. Except yourself. You'd be surprised: You do something incredibly clumsy on the court, like rapping yourself over the head with your racket or falling flat on your face, and you feel as if the whole world is having a good laugh. But most people never notice. I've never met a *real* tennis player who ever made fun of the way somebody else hit the ball. The only time people are really going to start watching you closely is when you start hitting the ball bloody well. Then you enjoy it.

Rod. Another thing you don't want to do is to keep looking over your shoulder all the time, trying to measure your progress with others who may have taken up the game at the same time. Everybody advances at his own pace in tennis; that's one of the great things about the game. If you're a good athlete to start with, and if you're in good shape, you're going to pick up the game quicker than somebody who isn't so well coordinated or is so out of shape he gets tired when he goes to tie his shoelace. Still, being a good athlete doesn't have to have anything to do with having fun at the game. From what I've been able to see at our Tennis Holidays, the "better" players don't necessarily enjoy themselves more than the beginners.

Roy. Not at all. The first year we ran one of our Tennis Holidays in New Hampshire, we had a woman in her late fifties. I'll never forget her. Not only was she a complete beginner, she was one of the most poorly coordi-nated women I'd ever seen. None of us could figure out at first just what the deuce she was doing trying to play tennis.

Rod. I remember her. If I had her determination I probably would be undefeated in tennis.

Roy. Either undefeated or *dead*. She *was* determined, and we kept working with her, and damned if by the third or fourth day, she wasn't getting the ball over the net a few times. Okay, this woman is never going to be a Margaret Court, a Billie Jean King or a Chris Evert, but she'd come a *long, long* way herself. I don't think to this day we've ever had a person go home in a happier frame of mind, feeling better about herself.

Rod. That's the key, really; keeping things within your own perspective. The players who have the most trouble enjoying tennis are players who constantly expect too much of themselves. I know because I was that way when I was younger. I couldn't stand to lose a point, let alone a game, a set, or a match. As long as I was winning, I was in a good enough mood, but when I'd start to lose, I'd get moody, and it would take a good friend like Emmo or, later, my wife, Mary, to tell me that I was acting like a bloody pain in the behind. Now, when I go out to play a match, I give it everything I have. If it's not enough, well, that's the way it goes, and I'm not going to let it get me down. In fact, I can honestly say that I enjoy myself more when I play tournament tennis today than I did when I was the number-one-ranked player. Then every time I went out on the court I felt as if I was defending the universe. The pressure was always there. Now when I go out to play I don't have to think about that anymore—I just play to play. I still try to win, and I still enjoy winning, but the pressure against losing is gone and that makes it all the easier.

Roy. I feel pretty much the same way. Then again, maybe I've had a little more practice at it than Rocket. But one thing I've come to realize now that I'm a little older and have a slightly different perspective on the game is that there is far more to tennis than winning matches and winning tournaments. Tennis is one of the few sports you can enjoy at so many levels. I'll always enjoy good competitive tennis, but there are other sides to the game. A nice, relaxed game of social mixed doubles is fun. So is a doubles game with some young kids playing. Just getting out on a court and hitting is fun. In all these situations you don't have to concentrate as hard as you normally do, you're not as tense as you are in a tournament. You can kid around a little, have a few good laughs. Tennis can be a terrifically social sport if people approach it the right way. On the other hand, if you take your tennis so seriously that the only way you can enjoy it is to play a match in a tournament, you're missing out on a lot.

Rod. Not that you can't have fun playing tournaments, too. Here, again, it's a matter of attitude. If you enter a local tournament with only one thought in mind—winning—you may well win, but you're so much better off going into a tournament with the idea that you're going to enjoy the challenge, play your best, and then look forward to the next tournament if your best isn't good enough. Whatever you do, you shouldn't get down on yourself every time you lose. Accept the fact that no matter how good you get, you're fre-

quently going to play against somebody who, on this particular day, is playing better than you. Also accept the fact that you're going to run into some days when you can't hit a ball to save your life. I remember a match I played once against Bjorn Borg, in Spain, when I simply couldn't keep a single ball on the court. Borg just ran through me. Don't ask me what I was doing wrong because I won't be able to tell you. All I know is that for some reason it dawned on me during that match that I couldn't hit the ball where I wanted to. Naturally, I lost, but whatever the problem was, it went away. The next day I played doubles and things were back to normal.

Roy. On one day, off the next; it's one of the fascinating things about tennis that nobody can figure out. And it's more the case for beginners. If you're just starting out at tennis, keep in mind that you're going to hit your share of great shots and lousy shots. Enjoy the great ones. Forget about the lousy ones, unless you can learn from them. And never take yourself too seriously. There is no way you can remind yourself too much of the fact that tennis is only a game, just a bloody game.

GETTING INTO GEAR

Rod. Having the right sort of gear—and I'm talking now about everything from the racket to the shoes to the type of clothes you wear on the court—can have a lot to do with how much you enjoy the game of tennis. But you can carry a good thing too far. I'm beginning to think that too many people now worry too much about how they *look* on a tennis court and not enough about how well they play.

Roy. I go along with that, particularly when you start talking about tennis rackets. Whenever I see people forking over $100 or more for some flashy new racket, I think about one of my boyhood heroes, John Bromwich. Bromwich was a great, great player—a

"touch" player, with fantastic control. And yet, he used the same old racket year after year after year. What a racket! The paint was peeling, and you couldn't even read the Slazenger label on it. The gut was frayed and so loose he could have used it for catching fish. That didn't make the Slazenger people too happy since they were paying Bromwich to endorse the racket. Finally, one day, they got him to play with a new one.

So, there he was playing Ken McGregor in a big afternoon match outdoors in Melbourne, using the new racket and running through McGregor, a great player himself. Bromwich won the first two sets without McGregor winning a game and was ahead some-

thing like 3–love in the final set when he hit a passing shot that landed about two inches out. That shot gave McGregor his first game.

So what did Bromwich do? He stormed over to the sideline, threw the racket down in disgust and said, "Bloody new racket! I can't play with it. It has no feel." And he finished out the match with his old one.

Rod. There are a lot of great John Bromwich stories. Vic Seixas likes to tell about the afternoon in England he was playing Bromwich on clay. Vic was never too confident on clay and he didn't figure to have much of a chance against Bromwich, who was probably one of the steadiest players ever to play tennis. But when they were warming up, Bromwich broke a string in his racket. I don't think it broke, really; I think it just died. Vic says that John kept staring at the racket, as if it were a member of the family who was very sick. He got another racket but he played so sluggishly Vic beat him in straight sets.

Roy. Today, of course, it's different. Most tournament players come to a match with five or six rackets. It's rare to find a player who gets attached to a single racket, although when Rocket was younger he used to get very personally involved with his equipment. He strung his own racket and was so attached to it that he would sleep with it under his pillow. He says he doesn't do it anymore, but I have a feeling if it weren't for his wife he'd still be doing it.

Rod. I admit I used to fuss over my equipment more than some players. I always figured it was important to know as much as you could about the sport you're devoting your life to. Right now I'm interested in the new materials that they're using to manufacture rackets, although I'm wondering if here, too, things might not be getting out of hand. I know a lot of intermediate players who change rackets like television channels. A new racket comes out—something made out of a combination of wood and aluminum and fiberglass and maybe cow dung—and a player will go out and buy it, thinking it's going to make a world of difference in his game. It usually doesn't.

Roy. Still, it is confusing, particularly the wood/metal question. I guess the question we get asked more than any other when it comes to rackets is whether we recommend wood or metal for beginners. I've used both, and there's a case for each. The wood rackets, generally, are a little heavier, but a little easier to control. The ball doesn't fly off the racket the way it does off most metal rackets. Metal rackets tend to be a little lighter, whippier, and easier on the arm. You can get a little more pace on the ball with less effort.

Rod. Some of the really old blokes in the game, like Emmo and Muscles, have switched to metal. They figure it has kept them in the game a few years longer. Considering all the trouble I've had with Muscles over the past couple of years, I sometimes wish the guy who invented metal rackets had gone into some other line of work. I've gone back to wood because it suits my game a little better. I get a better "feel" for the ball. But I don't think the feel is going to make too much difference to the average player.

Roy. I switched from wood to metal a few years ago, and I've stuck with it. Then again, I'm one of the "old blokes" Rocket is talking about. After all, I'm nearly *two years* older than he is. The metal gives me a little more pace on my serve, and when it comes to my serve, I'll take all the help I can get. John Newcombe says that his new metal racket helps *his* serve, which seems to me to be a good reason for outlawing it. Still, there might be some merit in what a lot of teaching professionals say: Starting out with a wood racket forces you to develop better basic stroking habits. In any case, what's happening now is that manufacturers are putting out wood rackets that play like metal and metal rackets that play like wood. The whole thing seems silly to me, especially when I see some of the price tags on these newer rackets. If I had asked my father for $100 to buy a new racket, he probably would have come after me with a pitchfork.

Rod. What it all comes down to in the final analysis is how each racket *feels* to you. Some rackets are heavier in the head than others.

This makes the racket a little whippier. A head-heavy racket can give you a little more power, but it also puts a little more strain on your elbow. I don't recommend head-heavy rackets for beginners. John Newcombe, on the other hand, *likes* a head-heavy racket, and so does Evonne Goolagong Cawley.

As far as the weight of the racket itself is concerned, here again it's a matter of personal preference. I find about 14 ounces a nice weight for me, which makes for a medium in most rackets. The racket Pancho Gonzalez used in his prime weighed only 13½ ounces. There's an Italian player, Beppi Merlo, who plays with a racket that's even lighter than rackets made especially for kids. He also strings it so loose you'd think it was an onion bag. When he was playing the circuit, he could drive you nuts with his angle and dink shots. Then there's Don Budge. His racket weighed 16 ounces. Then again, that's not a racket. That's a bloody war club!

Roy. Heavier rackets, generally speaking, are losing their appeal. There's a lot more volleying in tennis today than there was twenty years ago, and when you're spending a lot of time at the net, you're interested more in maneuverability—being able to move the racket back and forth quickly—than in heft.

Rod. But light or heavy, you want to make sure that you buy a racket with the right size grip for you. If the grip is too big, you're going to have trouble holding on to the racket, especially in hot weather. If it's too small, it may cause you blisters. And don't think blisters aren't a problem. Pancho Gonzalez, even after he'd been playing for years and years, used to get them. It cost him some big matches. I tend to experiment a lot with the size of my grips. You can increase the size of the grip by adding a little bit of tape to the wood before putting on the leather grip. If I'm hitting short and netting a lot of balls, I'll enlarge the grip, but then, if I start hitting long I'll bring it back down again. I find, generally, that my topspin shots work better with a smaller grip. But these are only personal things—things that work for me.

Roy. As far as your other gear is concerned, our recommendation is to use common sense, to stay within your budget, and to be more concerned with functionality than with style. A lot of people complain about clubs that have fairly strict standards about what you should or shouldn't wear, but there's a reason for it. Maybe it's just the way most of us in the game have been conditioned, but I don't like to see people playing tennis in jeans and in bathing suits. Besides, it's uncomfortable playing in clothes that weren't designed for tennis. Of course, the standards aren't as rigid as they used to be. Colors and stripes in tennis clothes are pretty much accepted now in all but a few clubs that still demand all white. In most places you can get by with almost any color as long as you're dressed in clothes that were designed for tennis.

Rod. I like the colors myself. I like looking fresh and sharp when I play and, in a funny way, I think it helps your game if you're dressed well and shaved. Most of the players I admired in my youth always looked good on the court. I remember Frank Sedgman and Ken McGregor. They didn't dress in the colors, but you never saw them look sloppy on the court. Most of the players today are the same way. The last time I saw Fred Stolle play, he was color-coordinated down to his socks. We get people like that at our Tennis Holidays all the time, so much so that we're thinking of instituting a special award— maybe we'll call it the Christian Dior award —for the sharpest dresser. Sometimes we even get husbands and wives in matching outfits. Now *that's* my idea of togetherness.

Roy. Togetherness indeed, but it's easy to get carried away with tennis clothes. Tennis, after all, is still a sport, not a fashion show. If the stripe on your headband doesn't happen to blend well with the stripe on your socks or your wristlet, and if the color of your shoe-laces doesn't match the color of the band inside your hat, nobody is going to drum you out of the game and I doubt if it's going to have any effect on your backhand. How the clothes *feel* is more important than how they look. Some of the newer dresses are very sexy, but a lot of the women who wear them are self-conscious about bending over. Then you get the men players who like to wear tight shorts because they look sharper, never mind that you can be a lot more comfortable and move a lot more easily if your shorts are *not* tight.

Rod. And while you're assembling a tennis wardrobe, don't overlook the accessories, particularly a sweater or warm-up suit. It doesn't have to be expensive, but a sweater or warm-up jacket can go a long way to prevent muscle pulls and strains. I know because I've had my share. You're much more susceptible to a muscle injury when it's cool than when it's warm. A jacket or sweater can also help keep your arm warm.

Roy. Hats are worth talking about, too. Growing up in Australia, where you sometimes play in 100-degree temperatures, hats are pretty much a necessity, but not every player finds them comfortable. I've always admired the billed cap that Frew McMillan wears, but lately, I don't wear a hat myself; my hair is a little too long. Rocket, though, has always liked them. When he was younger he used to line his hats with cabbage leaves, which I personally thought was disgusting. He doesn't do it anymore. I think the cabbage started to get to his brain. Or vice versa.

Rod. Not true. I may have used some cabbage once or twice, but that's as many times as you have to do anything in this world to get people talking. Anyway, the heat doesn't seem to bother me as much as it once did. It's the cool weather that worries me now. That's what age will do to you.

Getting into Gear: A Checklist

No one has yet proved that your ability to hit a tennis ball or your capacity for enjoyment is related in any way to the labels inside your tennis clothes or to the insignia on your racket. The best policy is to use common sense and to stay within your budget. If in doubt, patronize a shop that specializes in tennis or consult your local pro. Here are some tips:

1. Don't Overspend for Your First Racket

Spending $50 or more for a tennis racket in the beginning isn't going to help you learn the game any faster. There are a number of good rackets on the market—wood and metal —that sell for around $25 unstrung. All of them are serviceable. When getting the racket strung, use nylon instead of gut. Nylon is cheaper and more durable. Gut strings give you a little more pace and a little more feel, but only advanced players can tell the difference.

2. Select the Racket Weight That's Right for You

Most racket models come in light, medium, or heavy, but the terms are not standardized in the industry. A "light" racket from one company may weigh more than a medium racket from another company. "Light" rackets usually weigh 12 to 13 ounces, medium rackets 13 to 14 ounces, and heavy rackets 14 ounces or more. The best way to tell which size racket is best for you is to swing several different models and to pick the one that feels the most comfortable.

3. Pick the Grip Size with Care

Any experienced salesman or teaching professional should be able to select a racket grip that's geared to your hand. Racket grip sizes range from 4⅜ to 5 inches. If a grip is too big for your hand, you'll have trouble holding on to the racket. If the grip is too small, blisters may develop. A generally reliable rule of thumb (pardon the pun) is to get the size grip that allows you to wrap your hand around it with just enough room between the end of the middle finger and the heel of the thumb so that you can insert your pinky.

4. Be Careful About Footwear

Next to a tennis racket, a tennis player's closest friends are his two feet. If you can't move well, you can't play tennis well. When buying tennis shoes, concern yourself more with fit than with anything else. There are two types of tennis sneakers now available: leather and canvas. The leather shoes are more durable but also heavier and slightly hotter. Check the bottoms; certain bottoms lend themselves to certain surfaces. (A completely smooth bottom, for instance, will make running difficult on a clay surface.) Some bottoms are prohibited on certain surfaces. And don't take tennis socks for granted. Wear only socks designed for athletic use— heavy and absorbent. Many players wear two pairs of socks, especially on hard surfaces and hot days. No argyles, please.

5. Look for Functionality in Other Tennis Clothes

Clothes made especially for tennis are usually lightweight and absorbent. Cotton remains the best material, but some of the newer blends are nearly as good. Prices vary widely, according to style, workmanship, and the name on the label. Tennis shirts, shorts, and dresses with recognizable emblems may give you status on the court, but won't necessarily wear longer than tennis clothes without such emblems.

6. Go Easy on the Accessories

It's easy to get carried away with tennis accessories, given the ever-expanding number of tennis-related clothing items now on the market. For basics (beyond the standard wardrobe), get a sweater or warm-up jacket (warm-up pants are a good idea, too, but not as important as the jacket). Wristlets, headbands, and hats are not expensive and can come in handy in hot weather. Gloves are another story: Most professionals stay away from them because they take away from the feel of the strokes. If, however, your hands sweat profusely, a glove might not be a bad idea.

GETTING INSTRUCTION

Rod. Learning how to play tennis is just like learning how to do a lot of other things: the best thing is to develop good habits and proper techniques as early as possible, before you've had a chance to pick up bad habits.

Roy. We see it all the time at our Tennis Holidays: good players who want to get better but can't because they've got some very fundamental problems in their stroking technique. Before we can *learn* them anything, we have to *unlearn* them.

Rod. Not that it's impossible to become a tennis player on your own; Pancho Gonzalez at first had no formal instruction, and he certainly did okay for himself. Bjorn Borg never had any formal instruction when he started playing, either, although he'd played a lot of table tennis. But these guys are the exceptions. Most of the top players, at one time or another in their careers, have had somebody work with them intensively and individually on a day-in and day-out basis, instructing, drilling, stressing the fundamentals over and over. In my situation, it was a man named Charlie Hollis, who not only coached me day in and day out about tennis but even drilled me on what fork to use at the table.

Roy. There's always more to learn in this game, no matter how long you've been playing. Whenever a bunch of us Aussies get together for some team event, like the Davis Cup or the World Cup, you'd almost think we were beginners the way we tear down each other's strokes. Muscles will notice something I'm doing a little different on my forehand. I might give him a suggestion or two on his serve. Newk and Fred Stolle will help each other out, and we'll even give Rod's game a good working over. I remember once making a suggestion to Rod before a match he was scheduled to play against me: I told him he might do better if he closed his eyes when he went to hit his backhand. But he didn't listen. He's stubborn that way.

Rod. Not everybody is as lucky as I am to have a friend like Emmo looking out for my welfare. Tennis instruction isn't cheap, and that's why it's good to see more and more tennis clubs in the United States setting up junior programs so that kids whose parents can't afford private instruction have a chance to develop. If you're older, it's different: If you want instruction, you're going to have to pay for it. In some places, it can get expensive. It's up to you whether you want to spend the money or not, but if you're going to take lessons eventually, take them at the beginning, not after you've taught yourself.

Roy. Getting a good instructor can make a difference, not only in the way you play, but in your attitude toward the game. There are lots of good tennis players who are not very good teachers. They'd rather be out playing tournaments, not working with beginners. Besides, they take it too seriously, as if they were training you to be a doctor instead of a tennis player. When we hire pros for our Tennis Holidays, we don't particularly care about the tournament record of each pro. We want somebody, obviously, who can hit the ball, but mainly we want somebody who knows how to teach, who *likes* to teach, and who's good for a few laughs when we're having some beers afterward.

Enjoying it—that's the important thing. I like teaching tennis because I like people. I like meeting new people. I like to see people having a good time. It makes me feel better about life in general.

Rod. You can usually tell, just by watching the way a teaching pro relates to his students or even by sitting down and chatting with him about tennis, how he feels about teaching. If he—or she—grumbles and complains and gives you the feeling that he's doing you the greatest favor in the world by teaching you, look for somebody else. Look for somebody who really cares. We complained a lot when we were younger about how hard Harry Hopman used to work us, but we knew that Hoppy loved his work and cared about us, even though he had a funny way of showing it sometimes.

Roy. A bloody funny way. Like the time Lew Hoad nearly broke his neck trying to retrieve a ball in a Davis Cup match he was losing. There was Hoady just lying there, and none of us knew how hurt he was. Hopman stood up and threw a towel on the court, the way they do in a prizefight. Hoady saw the towel, burst out laughing, and went on to win the match.

Rod. Once you find a pro you like, stick with him for a while. It's silly to take a lot of lessons in the beginning from a lot of different pros. Most theories about hitting the ball are

Rock Valley College - ERC

pretty much the same when you come down to it, but there are enough individual difference in approach to make it confusing for a beginner. And don't turn your nose up at group instruction. Group instruction is much less expensive than individual instruction, and with the right instructor and the right group, it can be just as beneficial.

Roy. Maybe even more so. I've heard of places in New York that specialize in co-ed group instruction. They use tennis simply as a way of getting people together. (It almost makes me want to be a beginner again.) The one thing you have to be careful about when you're shopping around for group instruction is the number of people in each group. If you have to share a court and instructor with nine or ten other people, you're not going to learn much and you just might get yourself killed by some swinging racket. Our system at the Tennis Holidays is to limit the number of people in each group to four. Four students for each court for each instructor. And if they're co-ed, so much the better. I mean, you can't play tennis all day *and* all night.

TENNIS CAMPS AND CLINICS

Rod. It's obvious, since we have a company specializing in tennis vacations that emphasize instruction, that we reckon three days or a week of steady work on your game is going to do you some good, not to mention the good time you'll have while you're learning. The obvious advantage of any clinic-type program—ours or anybody else's—is that you're getting concentrated instruction during a time when you're not thinking about anything else but tennis. Sure, you can take instruction in your home club or park, but the minute you're finished you've got your job or your family or your house or your car to start thinking about. At a tennis camp, you can really lose yourself in the game.

Roy. People ask us all the time how much you can actually improve during three or six days of constant drills and instruction, and the answer we give is always the same: It's an individual thing. There's no use pretending otherwise: You can't become a tennis player in three days, or a week, or even a few months. But what you can get out of concentrated instruction is a solid foundation, something to keep in mind when you go back and start to work on your game on your own. It's safe to say the people who've come to a Tennis Holiday as beginners have picked up more in the few days they spend with us than they could have picked up in a few months on their own.

STAYING HEALTHY

Rod. Most of us who've been playing tennis nearly all of our lives have had our share of minor injuries, mostly sore arms and backs. But one of the best things about tennis is that really serious injuries are pretty rare. The workaday problems you have to worry about are things like muscles pulls, sprains, blisters, and that whole mysterious category of ailments called tennis elbow.

I've got an additional problem: sinus. It bothers me in cold, dry weather. In Hartford, during the 1975 World Cup, it got so bad that my nose started to bleed the night before I was scheduled to play Arthur Ashe. It also started bleeding during the match, and at a silly time, too: right in the middle of the tie-breaker in the second set. I think it bothered Arthur more than me because a couple of times when he was getting ready to serve, I had to walk away and tilt my head. It's lucky for me I won that tie-breaker since it gave me the set and meant I didn't have to play Arthur in the third set with a nosebleed to worry about.

Roy. It was better for *everybody,* considering Rocket's nose. But a nosebleed isn't the sort of injury the average player has to worry about. Your main worry is not to overdo it if you're not warmed up or not in good shape. If you have the sort of job where you're at a desk all week long and can only get out and play tennis once or twice on the weekend, for only an hour, don't be in a hurry to start hitting the ball hard. Hitting hard when you're not warm is the easiest way I know to get a sore arm. If you can manage the time, get some exercising in during the week—enough to keep you fairly limber for your weekend games, even a few minutes a day of simple stretching exercises, like the ones we talk about in the last chapter of the book. If you can't exercise, at least give yourself some time to warm up before you start hitting the ball hard.

Rod. The warm-up is important not only for the now-and-then player. Even if you play tennis every day, you should get into the habit of starting out slowly. It's especially important for me, since I've had trouble with my arm and elbow for years. If I start to hit out before I'm good and loose, I know I'm going to pay for it later that night. One of the habits I've gotten into—and something I recommend to other players—is always to wear a warm-up jacket. And always wait a while before you start banging serves and overheads. Those are the strokes that can do the most damage if your arm isn't ready for them.

Roy. Another big help in avoiding injuries is learning the proper way to hit the ball and to move on the court. Tennis is more a game of rhythm and balance than a game of strength.

The players that try to get by by muscling the ball are almost always the players who get the most injuries. The players who move well, who swing smoothly and with fluency and use their body weight well, who don't fight their bodies when they meet the ball— these are the players who hardly ever get injured. Rosewall, for instance, almost never gets hurt, and he works as hard as anybody on the court. And Pancho Segura has had only one injury in his entire career.

Rod. Emmo is the best example of the value of fitness I can think of. The way Hopman used to work us into what he considered good playing shape, most of us were so exhausted by the time the session was over we were lucky to crawl back to the showers. But there was Emmo, running an extra lap or two, or doing a few more dozen kangaroo hops. Maybe it was milking all those cows when he was younger. In any event, I don't think there's ever been anybody stronger in tennis than Emmo.

Roy. You try to work with what you have. I was never that confident about all my strokes, but I had my sound body, and I always felt that if I could get an opponent into the fifth set there was no way I was going to lose. I certainly wasn't going to lose any match because of fatigue. But even if you have the most fluent strokes, and even if you're in tip-top shape, you still want always to use some good old-fashioned common sense. If it's a very hot day, take it a little easier than you normally do. Maybe play some doubles or practice your strokes instead of trying to get in three hard sets of singles. You can get heat exhaustion at any age. And if you should feel yourself getting a little fatigued, dizzy, or nauseated because of the heat, don't try to be a hero. Take a little break. Sip some water or juice. Sit in the shade awhile. Write a poem. Or do what the Italian player Fausto Gardini used to do: Just dunk your head in an ice bucket. Do anything, but wait until you feel better before you start to play again. Social tennis is not show business. The show doesn't always have to go on.

Rod. Look who's talking. Emmo is forgetting about his Wimbledon match against Owen Davidson in 1965.

Roy. I'd like to forget that match. There I am, ahead by one set and about to break Dave-O on his serve in the second game, when he hits a drop shot that I really didn't have a chance for but tried to get to anyway. I ended up crashing my shoulder into the umpire's stand.

Rod. What some people won't do to attract attention. Lucky for Emmo it wasn't his right shoulder.

Roy. Lucky, my bloody foot! The shoulder was dislocated. I finished out the match, but couldn't keep up with Dave-O, who, by the way, was playing very well. Still, I'd like to have had that point back.

Rod. But that's an understandable injury. The kind of injuries you want to go out of your way to avoid are the ones that occur because of plain old stupidity. Somebody at one of our Tennis Holidays told the story of a guy he knew who had his own court and had a ball machine. This fellow had a little game he liked to play with the machine: He'd load it up, turn it on, and then take a running leap over the net to see if he could beat the first ball over. One day he didn't quite make it. His foot got caught in the net and he broke his ankle in two places. The only thing I could think of when I heard that story was this poor guy lying there on the court with the ball machine spitting balls out every few seconds. You don't get much sympathy from a ball machine.

Staying Healthy: A Checklist

Tennis is by no means a dangerous sport, but there is an injury factor all the same. Fortunately, most of the injuries are preventable, providing you use a reasonable amount of good judgment. Some of the things to bear in mind:

1. Always Start Slow

Regardless of whether you play once a day or once a week, give yourself time to get your muscles loose and warm before you start swinging hard. Some basic stretching exercises and a lap or two around the court can help you warm up more quickly.

2. Wear a Warm-up Jacket or Sweater

Even in warm weather, it's a good idea to keep a jacket or sweater on until your arm is good and warm. Slip it on afterward, too, particularly if you're going from an outdoor court on a hot day into an air-conditioned clubhouse.

3. Learn the Proper Stroking Techniques

Most muscle and elbow injuries among intermediate players result from improper stroking techniques: too much arm and elbow and not enough body weight in the stroke. A few lessons in the beginning can save you a lot of pain later on.

4. Be Wary of Court Conditions

Tennis is a fair-weather game. You should never play on any court unless it's completely dry. Be especially careful about damp spots on hard-surface courts.

5. Don't Overdo It

You know—or should know—better than anybody your limitations, and if you're over thirty-five don't make a habit of going beyond them. Go easy on hot days. And don't play for long periods of time if you have muscle trouble. You'll only aggravate the injury. Pace yourself in a match. Rest a little during the time you're changing sides (the pros do it, why not you?).

6. Get Into Shape

The better all-around physical shape you're in, the slimmer your chances of get-ting an injury. If you can only find the time to play tennis on the weekends, try to work in a little exercising during the week. Jogging, or running in place, is an excellent condi-tioner. So is jumping rope. A few stretching exercises and some basic calisthenics help, too. They will not only cut down the injury factor but help your tennis as well.

TENNIS ETIQUETTE

Rod. When it comes to tennis etiquette, I'm from the old school. I believe in it very strongly. I think courtesy is an important part of the game. I think you can enjoy the game without showing disrespect for the people you're playing with or the people you're watching.

Roy. It's pretty much an ingrained part of the game as far as I'm concerned and as far as most of the players I know are concerned. It's true in other sports, too—especially in the Oriental martial arts: all that bowing and nodding before you start throwing each other across the room. We're not quite that violent in tennis, but mutual courtesy is fundamental to good tennis. Of course, it's possible to carry it a little far. I know some players who consider it disrespectful if you blink while they're serving. I believe in courtesy, and I also believe in having a good time. If I'm playing social tennis, I like to keep some chatter going. I like to have a few laughs, particularly if it's at Rocket's expense. But the problem here is drawing the line between what's fun for you and what's upsetting to the people around you. I guess the only solution is to get rich enough to afford your own private court. Then you can set your own rules. Play Elton John records, take off your clothes, do anything you bloody well please.

Rod. When you come down to it, tennis etiquette is really nothing more than showing the same consideration to the people you're playing with and the people around you that you expect yourself. This goes for before you start to play, after you play, and especially while you're playing. The general rule while you're playing is not to do anything outside the general parameters of the game that's likely to upset your opponent. For instance, you should never serve the ball until you've looked up and made sure your opponent is ready. The reason I mention this in particular is that once when I was playing Pancho Gonzalez in New York, he complained to me and to the referee that I was doing just that–quick-serving. I didn't think I was, and I certainly wasn't trying to do it intentionally. And I have a feeling that this was Pancho's way of getting me to break my concentration. Finally, I said to him: "If you think I'm serving too fast, don't hit it back, and we'll play a let." Pancho, incidentally, took a set from me 16–14, but I won the match.

Roy. One of the areas in which etiquette really assumes importance is the business of making calls. Except for major tournaments, tennis players act as their own referees. My philosophy, ever since I started playing, has been to give the other guy the benefit of the doubt on close calls. I reckon if I'm going to win, a couple of close calls aren't going to make any difference.

Rod. I agree. What I've found is that if you give the other guy a break, he'll usually do the same for you. I've also made it a policy—and most Australian players in the game today feel the same way—not to question linesmen's calls. You're going to get your share of good calls and bad calls so what's the use of getting worked up about it: If you start thinking too much about the linesman, you stop thinking about your game. If it gets to be a pattern, a lot of obviously bad calls, I may throw a few stares at the linesman, just to let him know I'm not very happy, but I'd never carry on the way some players do, which is to refuse to play unless a particular linesman is removed.

Roy. Naturally, it's a different thing if the person making all the bad calls happens to be the person you're playing against. It's not an easy situation. Lots of times, an "out" ball will look "in" to you from your side of the court. And lots of times the other player will want to win so badly that he actually judges an "in" ball as being "out." It doesn't help in these situations to question the calls. Nobody likes to be called a cheater. And it doesn't help to start making some dodgy calls yourself. That just aggravates the situation. If the player is a friend and somebody you want to continue playing with, you might talk about it afterward. Otherwise the best way to deal with a player who calls every close ball his own way is just not to play with him, or her, anymore.

Rod. We should also mention here the whole messy business of temper, because it's involved with tennis etiquette, too. Except for a couple of us—and Bob Hewitt comes to mind right away—the Australians who developed under Harry Hopman do a pretty good job of controlling their tempers on the court. You hardly ever see Newcombe or myself or Stolle or Emmo throw a racket. Muscles will sometimes drop his racket in disgust, but he doesn't blow up very often on the court. The one big exception is Bob Hewitt; he's really a mystery. He's one of the most likable, easy-going guys off the court, but he was always getting himself into trouble with his temper

when he was younger. In fact, some of the other players on the circuit used to do things to deliberately goad Hewitt on, knowing if they could get him mad enough, he'd blow his stack and lose the match.

Roy. That's what Hopman trained us to realize when we were younger: that anger doesn't help you play any better. When you do lose your temper, you're only hurting yourself. He didn't mind if you blew off a little steam every once in a while, as long as you kept it under control. Lew Hoad used to get furious with himself but rarely for more than a couple of seconds. I only know of a couple of players—Gonzalez, for one, and Connors—who seem to play better when they're mad. For just about everybody else, your game starts to go to pot the minute temperament gets out of hand.

Rod. Another big reason for learning how to control your temper is that if you lose control with a tennis racket in your hand, you're liable to hurt somebody.

Roy. I'll say. I saw Pancho Gonzalez get so angry with himself after losing a game once that he threw his racket all the way across the court like a frisbee. He didn't mean to, but the racket sailed right toward the woman who was working as net judge. If she hadn't lowered her head at the last second—and, by the way, she never saw it coming—she might have lost her head. So Pancho was lucky, and in a couple of ways. Right after he threw the racket, some guy in the stands started to get on him a little bit. Pancho didn't like what the guy was saying, so he went into the stands after him. Then the guy stood up. Pancho's a big guy, but this bloke was six inches bigger. Tennis players are better lovers than fighters, so I don't really blame Pancho for what he did next: He simply looked up at the guy and walked back on the court. He was still so angry, though, that he stomped off the court, and defaulted the match.

Rod. I don't blame him for walking away, either. We get paid for hitting tennis balls, not people. Some guys, like Ion Tiriac, of

Rumania, could probably do both, if they wanted. I've seen Tiriac put his fist through a locker. Roger Taylor once threw a punch in the locker room; it landed, but he broke his hand. He won the fight, but lost the war.

Roy. While we're at it, we should mention some of the tournament players who never seem to get upset on the court—the players who seem to enjoy themselves the most.

Rod. I can think of several. Vijay Amritraj, certainly. The Danish player, Jan Leschly, who didn't turn professional because he felt that playing for money would take away from his love of the game. And let's not forget Evonne Goolagong Cawley. She once told a reporter something that all tennis players should memorize. She said: "I go onto the court and play for the love of the game. I think about having fun and what a pleasure playing tennis is. That seems to relax me and allows me to concentrate on playing the best I'm able." Then there's Torben Ulrich, who gets more fun out of not just tennis but life than just about anybody I've ever known with the exception of Emmo. And then there are so many of the oldtimers—the guys who played the game before there was so much money involved.

Roy. One of the happiest, most easygoing guys I've ever known in tennis was Mervyn Rose, although maybe I shouldn't say such nice things about him considering some of the hell he used to put me through when I was the youngest player on the Australian team. Rosie was always looking to pull off some practical joke, which made him a lot of fun to travel with, providing you weren't the butt end of the joke. I remember the first time I went to Europe with the Australian team. I'd never been out of Australia and I was still pretty much a kid from the farm. Naturally, I did some shopping wherever we went. I bought a camera for myself in Germany, and bought some perfume for my mother in Paris.

So here we are on a plane from Paris to London and customs declarations are passed out. I didn't know what to do with it, so I asked Rose. That was my first mistake. Rose told me that I was asking for trouble if I declared the camera and perfume and that the best thing to do would be to conceal everything I had as best I could and not declare anything. He even told me how to do it: stuff the perfume in the pockets of my overcoat, put the camera around my neck, and put on my overcoat around the camera. What I didn't realize was that you didn't have to pay any tariff if you weren't English.

Now we're landing, and I've got this bulky overcoat on covering the camera and with the perfume in the pockets. There's only one problem. It's about 90 degrees out, and everybody else on the team is waiting in line in their shirtsleeves except for me. It wasn't as if I was *conspicuous* or anything. Pretty soon I notice Rose go up ahead and whisper to some of the other players, and before you know it everybody on the team is doubled up with laughter, and that's when it dawned on me that I was the pigeon. I laugh about it now, but I felt pretty stupid then.

Tennis Etiquette: A Checklist

Many people in tennis will judge you more by the way you conduct yourself when you're on or near a tennis court than by the way you play. And not without good reason. Snobbery apart, tennis is more fun when everyone has a basic respect for everyone else and when the game is played amid a spirit of easygoing sportsmanship and courtesy. That's all tennis etiquette really is, in the end: common courtesy. Here are some of the "rules" that deserve special mention.

1. Dress Appropriately

You may not see any purpose in the traditional patterns of tennis dress, but most people who play the game do. So you owe it to them, at least, to dress with reasonable appropriateness. In many tennis clubs and resorts, you won't have the choice. You'll either wear tennis clothes or you won't be permitted to play.

2. Show Consideration

In tennis, you benefit from your opponent's mistakes, but how you go about generating these mistakes is another matter. Good, solid tennis is one way. Gamesmanship—stalling, making gestures, etc.—and outright rudeness are others. The simple rule is to refrain from any sort of action, apart from the game itself, that might disrupt your opponent's concentration.

3. Play at a Reasonable Pace

Maybe it suits your style to recite a little mantra to yourself before every serve, but if it takes too long it's not fair to the other players. Neither is it fair to the other players if you serve before the receiver is ready.

4. Call Decisions Fairly

Cheating at tennis (either consciously or unconsciously) is a good way to win matches and lose friends. Giving the other player the benefit of the doubt on close calls can do wonders for the atmosphere on the court. Frequently, it will inspire the other player to do the same for you.

5. Don't Quibble with Your Opponent's Decisions

Questioning the judgment, the sight, the manhood, the womanhood, or the integrity of your opponent rarely solves anything and only makes for an uncomfortable atmosphere. If you think the other player is deliberately cheating, sweat out the match and simply decline the invitation to play the next time you're asked.

6. Be Courteous to the Players Next Door

Tennis etiquette doesn't begin and end on your own court—not when there are other players on other courts. Some simple things to remember: One, never walk across a court when a point is in play, even if you're walking well behind the baseline. Two, never ask players to retrieve a ball of yours when they're in the middle of a point. Three, retrieve stray balls from other courts graciously, and wait until the players know the ball is coming back before you return it. Just rolling the ball back can sometimes cause an injury if the other players don't notice it on the court.

7. Be Gracious

About everything. About paying for balls at least every other time. About buying drinks. About sharing in the cost of a rented court. About the way your partner played in doubles. About the way your opponent played.

SURVIVING THE EARLY DAYS

Rod. Probably the toughest part about being a beginner is finding somebody to hit with, somebody who can keep the ball in play long enough so that you can practice your strokes.

Roy. I can usually tell just by the facial expression on a person in tennis whites if he's a beginner or not. Beginners seem to have this look on their face that says, "Love me. Please." But it *is* a problem. You can find another beginner to hit with, but if neither of you can hit the ball, or worse, if there are four of you out there who can't hit, it's not going to do you much good. This is why lessons can be important in the early days; at least you're hitting with somebody who's getting the ball back. And if you can't afford a pro to hit with, the next best thing is to find a friend who will have enough patience to let you practice at his expense. I've heard of people who've actually gotten married in order to guarantee themselves good tennis partners.

Rod. There are alternatives to marriage. One thing a pair of beginners can do instead of getting married, and instead of getting out there and just hacking at the ball, is to feed each other balls underhand from the net. You take turns, one player tossing the ball underhand, from the net, and then the other player. Or two or three of you might pitch in and rent a ball machine for an hour. While one of you is hitting, the others can be out gathering up the balls.

Roy. Sounds romantic. But you don't necessarily need a partner to practice. A practice wall is a good thing to work with for basic stroking techniques. And those trainers with the ball attached to the long rubber band— they're helpful, too, although you have to be careful. The ball sometimes comes back so fast you could hurt yourself. Even standing by yourself on the tennis court—or on a driveway for that matter—and bouncing a ball and hitting it can help. Anything you can do to help groove the stroke, to help give you a feel of what it's like to hit the ball correctly, and anything you can do to help your agility, your speed, your endurance, or your balance —it's all going to help you get better at the game more quickly. Sooner or later, of course, you'll have to find an opponent and get some match experience, but in the beginning there are more important things than playing games.

Rod. Amen! Too many beginners are in too much of a hurry to go out and play games. Games are fun, but they're even more fun once the two of you or the four of you can get some rallies going. You can get more actual hits in ten or fifteen minutes of concentrated practice than you can sometimes get in an hour of doubles.

Roy. And it can be just as much fun, too. Most professionals spend more time drilling and practicing than they do playing actual matches. I enjoy a good practice session, the tougher the better. Some of the nicest memories I have in tennis are the practice sessions that Harry Hopman used to put us through when I was just a junior. Hopman worked us bloody hard, but none of us ever dreamed of dropping out. We practiced hard. If you were at the net and weren't alert, somebody on the other side of the net might just slam a ball right at you. And if you got hit, you didn't complain. But you damn well kept an eye open for some revenge.

Rod. I loved those practice sessions, too. And still do like practicing. When I was younger, I could hit balls for hours and hours on end, and never get bored. Today I don't get bored, I get tired. You get a great feeling when you're hitting the ball really well. The ball comes over the net looking as big as a soccer ball, and everything seems to be moving in slow motion. You feel as if there's nothing you can't do with the ball. You get confidence. You're loose, relaxed. Everything is working for you.

Roy. But let's not oversimplify. Practice can be a frustrating time, too, especially if you're in too much of a hurry to improve. Remember, it has taken all of us who play this game for a living years and years of constant play and constant practice to reach a point where hitting a tennis ball is almost second nature. There's far more to it than simply having a good stroke technique. The big difference between the very good player and the average player is the ability to "read" the ball as it's coming over the net. That means being able to tell from the spin of the ball, the pace on it, from the height of it over the net, *where* you have to move to, how *fast* you have to swing, and *what* you have to do with the

racket. It's not something you think about. It's something that after a long period of time becomes instinctive.

Rod. A *long* period of time. Years. Years of hitting and hitting and hitting. You may never reach this point in your own tennis, but you can still work toward it, and enjoy the challenge of working toward it. To me, this is the real joy of tennis—not playing better, but *getting* better. Seeing improvement in yourself. Hitting shots today that you couldn't hit last week. Knowing that you're getting better. *Feeling* it.

The Language of Tennis

Like most sports, tennis has its own language. Knowing how to speak the language will make you feel more comfortable in a tennis atmosphere and should make it easier for you to enjoy the game. Here's a list of the most commonly used tennis terms you'll be running into throughout the rest of this book and throughout the world, wherever tennis is played.

Ace. Any good serve that the returner cannot touch with his racket.

Advantage. The term frequently used when the game has gone one point beyond the "deuce" (see below) stage. In tournament tennis when the announcer says, "Advantage, Laver," it means that Laver needs only win one point to win the game. In social tennis, the term is usually shortened to "ad." If the server is ahead after the deuce point, you refer to the score as "ad in." If the server is behind, you call it "ad out."

Ad court. The side of the court to which the "ad in" or "ad out" point is always served. It will always be diagonally to the right of the server.

Alley. The three-foot-wide area of space between the doubles sideline and the singles sideline.

American twist. Not a dance, a *serve.* Its characteristics are that the ball clears the *net* with a high loop, dips down, and after bouncing, veers sharply to the left of the receiver (assuming the server is right-handed). It's the most difficult serve to master.

Approach shot. Any shot hit with the intention of moving close enough to the *net* so that the next shot can be *volleyed.*

Australian formation. A method of lining up for doubles in which both members of the serving team stand on the same side of the court, the server close to the center line and his partner more or less in front of him but in the forecourt. This formation forces the returner to hit the ball *down the line.*

Backcourt. The term used to describe the area of the court running from the baseline to the service line. See also **forecourt.**

Backhand. Any stroke hit with the back of the hand facing the net and with the hitting arm more or less across the body at the moment of impact. When used alone, it refers to the basic backhand groundstroke, hit, usually, from the baseline. Otherwise it is used to differentiate other strokes from the forehand version, as in, "backhand *volley,*" "backhand *lob,*" etc.

Backswing. The backward arc or swing you make with the racket before swinging it forward to meet the ball.

Baseline. The boundary line on the far side of each half of the court.

Block. A method of hitting the ball in which you simply stick the racket directly in the path of the ball. A block can be an effective shot when the ball has been hit at you with considerable pace.

Break. The term used when a player loses the game he has served. It's also known as a "service break."

Cannonball. A serve hit hard and without spin. Also known as a "flat" serve.

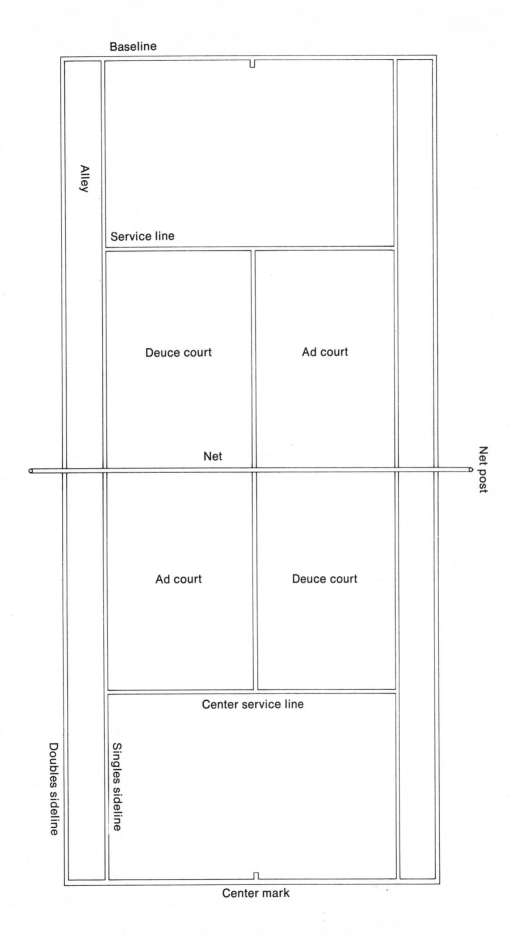

Carry. An illegal stroke in which the ball is held for a second or two on the racket and then thrown back, like a shot in lacrosse. If you carry the ball, you lose the point.

Chip shot. A groundstroke hit with an abbreviated motion and an angled *racket face*. It clears the net with underspin and when hit on a sharp angle, the way Laver sometimes hits it, it is an effective service return against big servers because it is a difficult shot to volley.

"Choke." To tighten up at a crucial point in a match.

Clay. Most people use this word to describe any number of dirtlike court surfaces, some of which are made of actual clay but others of which are granular surfaces called *en-tout-cas* or Har-Tru. Clay courts play slower than asphalt, grass, and cement courts.

Closed. There are two meanings for this term in tennis: One, it describes the relationship of the tennis racket head to the ball when contact is made with the strings in a position perpendicular to the ground—i.e., a closed angle. Two, it describes the body position when your feet and shoulders are facing the sidelines throughout the stroke. (See also "open.")

Continental grip. A method of gripping the racket in which the hand position is similar to that used to hold a hammer. The positioning of the wrist in this grip makes it easier to hit low-bouncing balls. The grip originally developed in Europe, where the clay surfaces yield a low bounce. Many professionals use this grip for serving and for hitting *volleys*. (See page 62).

Crosscourt. The term used to describe balls hit from one side of the court diagonally to the other side.

Deuce. The word describing the stage in a game when each player has won three points, and each time thereafter when the score is tied. Once a game has reached deuce, it takes two consecutive points from either side to win.

Deuce court. The side of the court to which the deuce point is always served. It will always be diagonally to the left of the server.

Dink. A soft little shot meant to clear the *net* and land short.

Double fault. The bane of tennis players at every level of competition: two successive *serves* that fail to land in the designated serving area. Your "reward" for double-faulting is that you lose the point.

Doubles. Tennis, two against two.

Down-the-line. The phrase that describes the route of a ball hit parallel to the sideline, as opposed to *crosscourt*.

Drive. A *forehand* or *backhand groundstroke* hit with a full *backswing* and a full *follow-through*.

Drop shot. A short *groundstroke*, similar to a *dink* but hit with pronounced *underspin*. It is designed to clear the net and have little or no forward movement after it bounces.

Drop volley. A *volley* hit with pronounced *underspin* so that it either bounces backward or has very little bounce at all.

Eastern grips. A system of gripping the racket for *forehand* and *backhand groundstrokes* that developed in the Eastern part of the United States. The telling factor in each *grip* is that the palm of the hand is in the same hitting plane as the racket head. (See page 56.)

Emmo. Roy Emerson's nickname.

Error. A term used frequently in tennis to describe a missed shot. There are two categories: "unforced errors," in which the missed shot presented no special difficulty to the player who hit it; and "forced errors," in which the missed shot occurred because of a very good return from the other player.

Fault. A serve that bounces outside the service box. (See *Double fault, Foot-fault.*)

"First one in." A method recreational players often use to start a game when a server is serving for the first time. The point doesn't take effect until the server gets a serve in the proper serving area, even if he serves 25 times. Thereafter, the normal rules prevail: two to a customer.

Flat serve. See *Cannonball*.

Follow-through. The finishing motion of a *stroke* once the ball has been hit.

Foot-fault. A serving transgression called whenever either of your feet touches the *service line* or beyond, or crosses the midline before the serve is actually hit. It's considered a normal *fault*, but is rarely enforced in recreational tennis.

Forecourt. The term used to describe the area of the court that runs from the service line to the net.

Forehand. Any stroke hit from the same side of the body as the hitting arm, with the palm facing forward during the stroke.

Game. (See page 44.)

Game point. A situation in which a single point can win a particular game, whether the score is 40–love, love–40, Ad-in, Ad-out, etc.

Grand Slam. Something that Rod Laver has won twice, making him the only man in history to do so. It's winning four major titles in the same year: The Australian, the French, Wimbledon, and the U.S. championships. Apart from Laver only three other players have done this: Don Budge, Maureen Connolly, and Margaret Court.

Grip. Two definitions: One, the leather covering at the butt end of the racket. Two, the way you position your hand on the racket.

Groove. To "groove" your strokes in tennis means to reach a point at which you're hitting the ball well without any real conscious thought.

Groundstroke. Any stroke, *backhand* or *forehand*, hit after the ball has bounced. *Drives*, *chips*, *lobs*, etc., are all groundstrokes.

Gut. A material from which some racket stringing is made.

Hacker. The typical struggling tennis player.

Half-volley. A stroke in which the ball is contacted the second it bounces, at about shoetop level. It is usually hit in self-defense when the return has landed at your feet.

Ladder. A posted roster of players at a club or park in which players are ranked (1, 2, 3, etc.) according to their performance record against other ladder players. A "ladder match" denotes a match in which a ladder ranking is at stake.

Let. Any call that results in a point being played over. A "let" serve, for instance, is one that hits the net before landing in the service box.

Lob. A groundstroke that clears the net by a very high margin, high enough, at least, to get over the head of any player at the net.

Lob volley. A rare stroke in tennis: a lob hit before the ball hit to you has bounced.

Long. A term used to describe a ball that has landed beyond the *baseline*.

Love. The tennis term for zero.

Match point. The stage in a tennis match when a single point will win the match for one of the players or teams.

Mixed doubles. Any doubles game in which there are both male and female players. Generally, the term is used to describe competition in which each side consists of a male and a female player.

Net. Your number-one opponent in tennis. It is three feet high in the middle and three feet, six inches high at each end.

No-man's-land. The court area that lies roughly between the *service line* and a yard or so inside the *baseline*. It's so called because when you're caught there, the returns tend to bounce at your feet, making your return extremely difficult.

Not up. A term used to call a play in which the ball has bounced twice before being hit.

Nylon. In tennis, a type of stringing that is cheaper than gut; it lasts longer but is not quite as responsive.

Open. Two uses: One, to describe the position of the body and feet with relation to the net—the more *toward* the *net*, the more "open." Two, to indicate the angle of the racket on contact. "Opening up" the *racket face* means canting it slightly clockwise from the *flat* position.

Overhead. A stroke, similar to the serve, used to hit a ball when it is above your head. Also known as "smash."

Pace. The speed of the ball.

Passing shot. A shot meant to elude a player either approaching or already at the net.

Percentage tennis. A loosely defined strategic approach to tennis in which you attempt to hit shots that strike a balance between defensive caution and offensive pressure.

Placement. A winning *groundstroke* or *volley* that eludes your opponent more by virtue

of where you aim it than by virtue of how hard you hit it.

Poaching. A term used in *doubles* describing the action of a player at the net who cuts across the court to intercept returns before they reach the backcourt.

Psyched up. Keyed up. Psychologically itching for action.

Putaway. Any shot in tennis in which the chances of making an error are very slight and the chances of your opponent returning the ball are even slighter.

Racket face. The strings of the racket.

Rally. A term frequently confused with *volley*. It applies to the sequence exchanges of shots across the net until the point is decided.

Ready position. The stance you assume when waiting for the ball.

Retriever. A type of player whose game is built totally around his ability to run down balls and return nearly all of them.

Rocket. Rod Laver's nickname, derived from his birthplace in Australia, Rockhampton.

Serve. The ball, hit in the air, that starts every point.

Serve and volley. A strategy in which the server follows his *serve* to *net* with the idea of *volleying* the return and forcing a quick resolution to the point.

Service line. The line running parallel to the *baseline* that establishes the lateral boundary of the service box. See court diagram.

Set. A completed group of games that comes to an end when one player or the other has won six (providing he leads by at least two), or when one player has won seven games, as opposed to five; or has won a tie-breaker (see below).

Set point. A stage in a match when one player (or team) or the other needs only one more point to win the set.

Set-up. See Sitter.

Sitter. A short, high-bouncing ball that presents the returner with an opportunity for an almost certain winner. Also known as a "set-up" or "putaway."

Slice. A stroke in which the racket face cuts down and behind the ball on contact imparting *underspin*.

Smash. See Overhead.

Sudden death. A term used to describe *tie-breakers* in which the outcome is decided after a fixed number of points. In the 9-point tie-breaker, for instance, the first player to win five points wins the set. Thus if each player has four points, the player winning the next point wins the set.

"Take two." In social tennis, a gracious offering from either side that allows the server a second chance at the first *serve*; whenever something unusual has happened to cause a fault or to cause a delay between first and second serves.

Tennis elbow. A fairly common and very painful elbow malady that affects tennis players at every level. It generally results from too much repeated stress on forearm muscles, which, in turn, affect the elbow joint.

Tie-breaker. A deciding "overtime" game played when a set has ended at 6–6. There are several versions: 9-point, 12-point, etc. See page 44 for clarification.

Topspin. Forward rotation of a tennis ball in flight. Balls hit with topspin tend to drop down, which means they can be hit harder and with more control.

Touch. Good racket control. A "touch" player is one who can hit a variety of shots.

Underspin. Backward rotation of a ball in flight. Balls hit with underspin tend to float more than balls hit with topspin, which means they must be hit more softly than an average shot. See *slice*.

Volley. Any ball, except the *serve* or *overhead smash*, hit before it bounces. Most volleys are hit near the *net*.

Western grip. A somewhat unorthodox way of gripping the racket that developed on the cement courts of California, where the ball has a characteristic high bounce. In this grip, the wrist is very nearly under the racket face.

Wood shot. A shot that is hit with a section of the racket other than the strings. The same term is used when a player is using a metal racket.

How to Keep Score

Points

You score a point in tennis anytime your opponent fails to return a ball you've hit within the boundaries of his court. It doesn't matter who is serving at the time, or how many times the ball goes over the net before this occurs. The first point you or your opponent wins is called "15." The second point is called "30." And the third point is called "40." The first person to win four points wins the "game" in tennis, with this condition: He has to win by two points. If the score is 40–30 and the person with 40 wins the next point, he wins the game. If the score is tied at 40, or, as it's referred to, "deuce," the game moves into a stage known as "ad." If the server leads by one point after deuce, the score is referred to as "ad in." If the server is behind at this point, the score is referred to as "ad out." Play continues until one player or the other has won by two points, no matter how many deuces come about.

Games, Sets, and Match

Once a game has been decided, the serve moves to the other side. It alternates every game thereafter. You continue to play games until one player has won six, or has won the "set," but, again, with a major condition. To win a set, you have to win by at least two games. Winning a game when the score is tied at 5 games all simply puts you ahead by one game; it doesn't win you the set. Years ago, and in many places still today, a set can sometimes go on for twenty games or more before one player gains a two-game edge. In professional tennis this is no longer the case: Once a set has reached the 6–6 stage, a special game, known as a tie-breaker, is played, and the winner of the tie-breaker is awarded the set. A tennis "match" is generally over when one player has won the best of three sets, but in important tournaments, it takes the best of five sets to win in men's singles events.

Tie-Breakers

There are several types of tie-breakers in vogue today. The most common form, used by World Championship Tennis (WCT), is the 9-point sudden-death tie-breaker, decided when one player or the other wins five points. WCT also uses, on occasion, the 13-point tie-breaker, a sudden-death affair that goes to the first player who wins seven points. Another tie-breaker version is the 12-point tie-breaker. Here the game goes to the first player to win seven points, providing he is two ahead of his opponent. In all tie-breakers the serve alternates back and forth. In the nine-point tie-breaker the player who would normally serve starts out by serving the first two points. Then the other player serves two points; at this stage, the players change sides. Player one then serves twice again (the second, only if needed), and, if necessary, the second has the last three serves. Should the score be tied 4–4, the player receiving the final serve (player one) has the right to select the side on which he wants to receive.

*Learning the Basic Techniques
(And We Mean Basic!)*

Eventually you conquer it, the trauma of your initial encounter with a tennis court. And when you do, if you're like most people, you begin to realize that there is a physical logic to the game. Swinging too late or too early, swinging up or swinging down, keeping the wrist too loose or too tight, following through too far or not following through enough—they all have a bearing on what the ball does after you make contact. Control the variables, you tell yourself, and you control the ball.

But which variables, and how much control? You seek help. And you get it. One professional tells you take a step before you hit the forehand. Another tells you to take a step while you hit the forehand. Another tells you not to take a step at all. Ask enough people and you'll probably get somebody to tell you to do the tango when you hit the ball. Who do you trust?

Rod. How do you hit a tennis ball? It's such a simple question, you'd think there was a simple answer, a single technique, systematic and easy to follow, like a recipe for a French soup.

Roy. Which, of course, is the way some teaching professionals approach the game. The wrong way, as far as I'm concerned.

Rod. As far as I'm concerned, too. Tennis is an individual game. You can get all the instruction you want, but in the final counting, you have to do what works best for you. There are a lot of things I do when I hit the ball that most people say you're not supposed to do. I put a lot of wrist into my strokes, and most teaching pros say you shouldn't. That's good advice for beginners, but wristy shots *work* for me. I don't think I would have had near the success I've enjoyed in my career if I had hit the ball the conventional way.

Roy. True. The whole guts of the situation is where you make contact with the ball and what you do after contact—a distance of no more than two feet. Everything else—the grips you use, the amount of backswing, the wrist, the position of the body—has its importance, too, but only insofar as it affects what happens when the racket meets the ball. When you're first learning this game, certain techniques make it easier to control the ball. And there are very logical reasons why they produce better results. If you're standing side-on to the net when you're hitting most strokes, for instance, you're going to be able to hit the ball with a lot more power and a lot more control than if you're facing front, because it will be easier to transfer your weight. For most people, that is. Still, in the final analysis, if you can hit the ball consistently *where* you want to and *how hard* you want to, I don't care if you're standing on your head when you hit, I'm not going to tamper with your style.

THE FUNDAMENTALS OF GOOD STROKING

Rod. Different techniques work best for different strokes, but there are some basic principles that pretty much apply to all the strokes in tennis. The three that we stress at our Tennis Holidays are footwork, watching the ball, and hitting "through" the ball.

Roy. It's difficult to say which of the three is most important, but the one most players don't think about enough is footwork. Almost every very good player moves well. This doesn't mean being lightning fast on your feet, but it does mean moving smoothly and with good balance. If you can move smoothly, you can set up your balance for each shot quickly. That's going to give you better control of your strokes. Good balance means good control. I've always figured that a person who's had a lot of ballet training would make a great tennis player.

Rod. Emmo Nureyev! That has a nice sound to it. And I agree. Most of the time if I'm not hitting the ball well, the problem is in my feet. I'm not moving them quickly enough, not getting set up for my shots quickly enough. That's when I start slapping and lunging at the ball, and making errors.

Roy. But when Rocket *is* playing well—and it's true for most players—feet are moving like pistons, even when he's back at the baseline waiting for a return. Rosewall is another. The big reason Muscles' strokes are so fluid is that he moves so gracefully.

Rod. He's never off-balance when he starts his stroke. He has beautiful body control. Chris Evert's another good example. The reason she hardly ever misses from the baseline is that her feet are always in good position for a smooth stroke.

Roy. Stopping and starting, shifting your weight quickly from one foot to another—if you can execute these movements smoothly, you've got a leg up on other beginners. So anything you can do to improve your basic balance and agility, whether it's skipping rope or doing special agility exercises like we'll show you later in the book, or studying karate or kung fu, or dancing on hot coals, your tennis is going to benefit.

Rod. Now let's talk about a second very basic *basic:* letting the racket do the work, letting the racket head always come *through* the stroke.

Roy. I like the way Rocket says "throooo." It really gets the point home. The tendency among most beginners is to shorten up as soon as they hit the ball. No good. The only way to control the stroke is to let the arm and racket flow through naturally, almost as if the ball had never been hit.

Rod. A good way to visualize what we mean by hitting "through" the ball is to think of a defensive halfback in football intercepting a pass on the run. If he's timed the interception well, he doesn't even break stride. That's how most tennis strokes should be hit. The racket intercepting the ball, moving through without *stopping*, and then directing the ball to wherever you want it to go.

Roy. Finally, let's touch briefly on one other basic—watching the ball.

Rod. It's such an obvious thing, you'd think that people who've been playing the game for years and years would do it as a matter of course. But it's amazing how many errors occur in a professional match because one of the players simply takes his eye off the ball.

Roy. Don't remind me. I almost blew a Wimbledon championship to Fred Stolle in 1964 because I took my eye off the ball on a crucial point. I'd won the first two sets 6–4, and 12–10, and had Stolle down love–40 on his serve in the first game of the third set. He hit a couple of good shots to come back to 30–40, but then I got him way out of position on a return of serve, and all I had to do was hit a simple forehand into this huge open court to win the game. Then, for some stupid reason, I took another quick look to see where Fred was, and I hit the ball into the net. He went on to win the game, and the set, and if Fred had been serving a little better—he double-faulted a couple of times in the first game of the fourth set—I might not have won it.

Rod. Emmo never gave me those "gifts" when we were younger. And that's what pointless errors at crucial times in a match really are—gifts. But watching the ball is really a matter of concentration. Constant concentration. What I try to do if I don't think I'm hitting the ball as well as I should be hitting it is to see the label on the ball as it's coming toward me and then to watch the ball actually coming off the strings.

Roy. I remember a woman player from Australia named Mary Hawton who went even further: She was so intent on watching the ball she would actually follow the ball with her eyes and then, instead of lifting her head to see where the ball was going, she'd continue to move her gaze back for a second. That way, she made certain that she wouldn't lift her head too soon. Billie Jean King tends to do the same thing on her backhand. Good golfers will do it, too.

Rod. I know one golfer who doesn't always do it; his name is Rod Laver. But it's a point that you can't stress enough in tennis. Watching the ball. You hear a lot of talk in this game about reflexes, but what passes for

quick reflexes is often nothing more than good concentration, mental alertness.

Roy. Watching the ball.

Rod. Watching the ball.

GROUNDSTROKES

Rod. One of the things Emmo and I have both learned from our Tennis Holidays experience is that most social tennis players could play tennis a lot better and enjoy themselves more in the process if they would just do one thing: solidify their groundstrokes. We see players all the time who have great serves and who volley well, but they still end up beating themselves because they make ridiculous errors from the baseline.

Roy. Part of the reason for this, I think, is that so many professionals today play the serve-and-volley game that some people have the notion that groundstrokes aren't that important. But this is going to change, now that so many tournaments are being played on slower surfaces indoors. Even Forest Hills has gone from grass to a much slower surface, Har-Tru. On a slow surface, a serve-and-volley game alone isn't enough. You have to be consistent from the baseline, and you have to be patient.

Rod. I'm happy about the change. I think tennis fans want to see longer rallies. I can get awfully bored watching a match in which every point is decided either on the serve or return of service. And it takes a pretty boring match to put me to sleep. But all the good younger players—Connors, Borg, Vilas—have excellent groundstrokes, and what we're going to see in tennis instruction over the next several years is less work on the volley and more on building a fundamentally sound baseline game.

Roy. Which will be like turning back the clock, because years ago groundstrokes were everything. I think of players like John Bromwich, who might have been one of the

steadiest players in the history of the game—the guy just never missed a groundstroke. Harry Hopman told me once about a Davis Cup match Brom played against Frank Parker. Now there was another groundstroke master, Parker. A machine they used to call him. Unbeatable from the baseline.

So they met for the first time in a Davis Cup match in 1939. During the warm-up, the ball went back and forth so many times without a miss that Bromwich finally kicked it aside; it had turned too green from the grass. When the match finally got started, the people in the stands figured Bromwich was out of his mind for trying to outduel Parker from the baseline. It was like trying to get running plays to work against those four monsters who played on the line for the Pittsburgh Steelers when they won the Super Bowl for the first time. It didn't matter. Parker said later he thought he'd played very consistently, but he still lost in three sets.

Rod. Most of the great Australian players had strong baseline games, especially Jack Crawford.

Roy. Crawford was unreal. I still remember how amazed I was the first time I saw him play. Here was a man who wasn't very strong, wasn't very athletic, and never hit the ball really hard. But he was so smooth, like poetry in motion. And he knew so much about tennis, and so much about the players he was up against, that he was hardly ever out of position. He'd hit the ball to one side of the court, and the other guy would run like a rat to get it. Then Jack would take a couple of steps, rarely more, and hit it on the other side of the court. And the guy would run like a rat to get to it. The match would go on like that until the other guy was sweating like a bloody pig, and there was Jack, in a long pair of creams, not a bead of sweat, just hitting the ball, in perfect control.

True, you have to do a little more than just hit the ball today the way Crawford did if you're going to get anywhere, but there's so much from a game like his that a beginner can learn. The secret to good groundstrokes isn't power, it's control. Control and consistency.

Rod. Why go all the way back to Crawford to prove the point? Look at Rosewall. Rosewall isn't a power player, but his groundstrokes are as sound as anybody's.

Roy. It's his precision that kills you. Rosewall can put the ball almost anywhere he wants to on the court, and from either side. When you've got that kind of control, you don't need power.

Rod. And when you don't have to rely so much on power and pace, you're not going to beat yourself with errors.

Roy. And where does that precision come from? Above all, from having a fundamentally sound stroking technique. Hitting with balance and smoothness and with the weight of your body always moving forward.

The Basics of the Forehand

The forehand Rod and Roy recommend to beginners is a simple, uncomplicated shot. The key to hitting the stroke is early preparation. Early preparation consists mainly of getting the body—particularly the shoulders—turned side-on to the net and getting the racket back as soon as possible. There is a slight loop to the backswing, recommended because it helps you in timing the stroke. The ball is hit flat, that is, with the strings perpendicular to the ground. The follow-through is up and out. Here are the key elements in sequence.

1. Start with Ready Position

The ready position is home base for the tennis player—the position you return to (or try to, at any rate) every time you stroke the ball and prepare to hit the next one. Roy, in the ready position, is alert but relaxed. His racket is held comfortably in front of the body. His front hand cradles the racket. His knees are slightly bent, and the racket head is cocked slightly above his wrist. Notice that he is not leaning back on his heels but is leaning forward in a slight crouch. From this position, he's ready to kick off in any direction.

Roy is *not* holding the racket very tightly at this stage—just firmly enough to keep it from falling. Holding the racket too tightly is a common mistake among beginners, and one of the reasons beginners get arm-weary after short hitting sessions. The grip in this ready position is midway between the Eastern forehand and the Eastern backhand (see below and page 56). The front hand will turn the racket into the proper grip position during the backswing.

2. Use the Eastern Forehand Grip

The Eastern forehand grip is sometimes called the "shake hands" grip. Guess why? It was developed on the clay courts in the East, where most balls bounce belt high. Hitting balls that bounce at this height with an Eastern forehand grip puts the palm and the wrist in the same hitting plane as the racket head. This means you don't have to maneuver the wrist to hit the ball "flat." To assume the Eastern forehand grip, put your hand flat against the strings. Then slide it down the handle without letting the racket turn in either direction. Once you reach the butt of the handle, let your fingers curl around the grip naturally, the fingers comfortably spread.

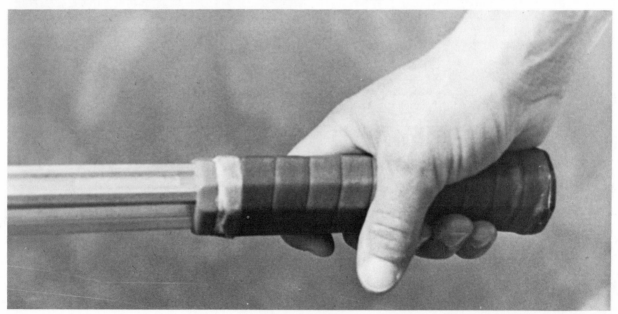

3. Turn Shoulders Early

The earlier you prepare yourself to hit any stroke in tennis, the better. Here is one of the fundamental commandments of tennis, and it wasn't written by Charlton Heston. Early preparation for the forehand means getting the shoulders turned and the body facing side-on and getting the racket back early—*before* the ball bounces. The easiest way to reach this position is to turn the shoulders, pivot on the foot *opposite* your hitting arm, and then step back with the other foot. Presto! You're side-on to the net. Roy's weight at this stage in the stroke is on the back foot. Notice that his elbow is slightly bent and fairly close to the body. Extending the elbow straight back restricts a free-and-easy stroking motion.

4. Meet the Ball in Front

It's not always possible, of course, but the swing on the forehand should be timed so that you're meeting the ball at a point just about even with the front foot, a comfortable arm's distance away from the body, belt high. The swing is rhythmic. It's a stroke, not a swipe. As Roy swings, his weight shifts from the back foot to the front foot. But, *it's the arm and racket that carry the weight along, and not vice versa.* His wrist is firm on contact. His eyes watch the ball as it leaves the racket strings.

5. Take a Full Follow-through

Roy is in the position you should be in once you've finished the basic forehand stroke. Getting here means allowing the racket and arm to flow through the ball, and slightly up. The "up" part is especially important; that's what gives the ball the necessary height to get it over the net. Notice that Roy's feet stay side-on throughout the stroke. Only the upper part of his body—the shoulders, chest, and hips—turn toward the front.

A FINAL LOOK

Roy. When you're first learning the forehand stroke, don't worry about hitting the ball hard, and don't worry too much about where the ball is going. Instead, get a sense of being ready for the shot, a sense of the body weight moving into the stroke, and of the arm and racket moving through the ball and out. Always check where you finish up after the stroke. That will give you a clue as to whether you're stroking the ball properly. Also, get into the habit early of hitting the ball so that it clears the net by at least three feet, even more. By hitting the ball high, you not only reduce the possibility of hitting the ball into the net, you also get more depth into your shot. And that's really the key to an effective forehand: depth. Once you get the ball over the net with reasonable consistency, you can start experimenting with direction. To hit a forehand down the line, you simply delay the stroke a fraction of a second, hitting it almost even with your hip. To hit it cross-court, you simply make contact a little sooner.

The Basics of the Backhand

The backhand that Rod and Roy teach to beginners is almost a carbon copy of the forehand, with only a couple of minor exceptions: the grip and the contact zone. The Eastern forehand grip doesn't work well for the backhand, because the palm and wrist are in *front* of the racket and it's difficult to generate power. The Eastern backhand grip puts a good portion of the palm and wrist behind the hitting plane. The contact zone of the backhand is slightly to the front of the forehand zone. Hitting the ball further in front enables you to take a fuller, freer swing. Once the ball gets too close to the body or behind you on the backhand side, the result is a cramped swing. And with all the problems in the world, who needs a cramped backhand swing? Here are the fundamentals:

1. Start with Ready Position

2. Use the Eastern Backhand Grip

To assume the Eastern backhand grip, start out with the Eastern forehand and rotate the racket approximately a quarter-turn clockwise. This should place the top left edge of the grip in the center of the "V" that's formed by your index finger and thumb.

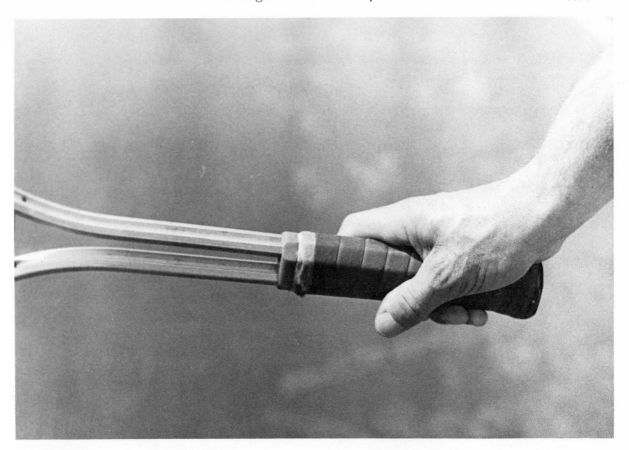

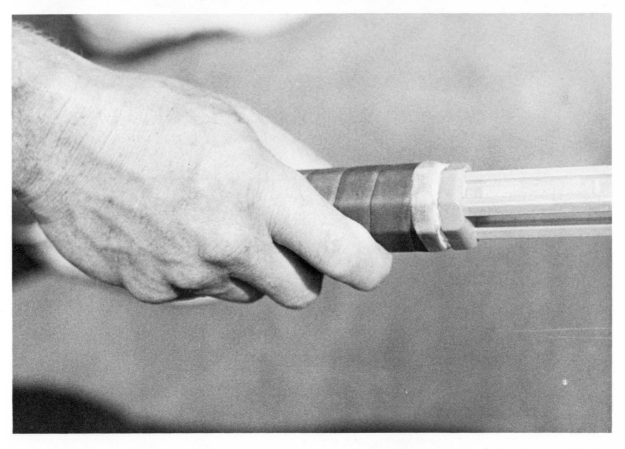

3. Turn Shoulders Early

From the ready position, Rod quickly turns his body side-on, pulling the racket back with his free hand. He pivots on the foot opposite his hitting arm, then takes a step back with his other foot. He's conscious of looking over his front shoulder. The racket is back. The racket head is above the wrist, and the elbow is bent, almost touching his body. His weight is slightly on the back foot. He's alert but relaxed.

4. Make Contact Early

Rod makes contact with the ball about a foot in front of his front foot. Notice that the elbow is still tucked fairly close to the body. Getting the elbow too high on the backhand is a common habit among beginners. Another common habit is opening up the body too soon. Rod's weight is moving forward into the stroke, but his shoulders do not begin to move forward until the racket has begun the follow-through.

5. Take a Full Follow-through

The key to the backhand follow-through is letting the racket head lead the arm and shoulder, and not vice-versa. The elbow stays close to the body until the pull of the racket forces it out. When you finish the follow-through, the racket head should be above the wrist and slightly higher than eye level.

A FINAL LOOK

Rod. Getting that front shoulder turned well around, and keeping your elbow in: concentrate on these two details and you'll save yourself a lot of grief on the backhand. If you can't get any muscle into the stroke, keep your free hand on the racket a little longer. If you're really having trouble, experiment with a two-handed grip. Neither Roy nor I recommend the two-handed grip; it cuts down on your reach. But some awfully tough players use it successfully, and who are we to argue with success? Above all, develop a sense of the racket head and the arm leading the body weight. Your weight is moving forward, but it's following the racket head, not the other way around.

THE VOLLEY

Rod. Emmo and I both have a special feeling for the volley. The national hero in Australia at the time we were first breaking into the game was Frank Sedgman, who had one of the best volleys of all time.

Roy. It was his best shot. The main reason, I guess, was that he was such a great natural athlete. Technically, there's nothing very complicated about the volley. It's more a quick jab than a stroke. Quickness and good reflexes are mainly what it takes to be a good volleyer, and Sedgman had both. He played cricket and football in school. He was a hurdler. He played a lot of basketball in the winter. He was one of the most agile tennis players I've ever seen.

Rod. Probably the main reason Sedgman volleyed so well was that he learned to volley before he learned to hit groundstrokes. He first fooled around with tennis by hitting the ball against the barn where he lived. Because the ground was so choppy the only way he could get any rallies going with himself was to hit the ball before it bounced. I imagine there were some animal droppings around, too, and maybe that's why he became so agile: learning to hit the ball without getting his feet in the muck.

Roy. Very possible. Agility *is* the key to good volleying. Agility, confidence, and aggressiveness. This is what Harry Hopman taught all of us, and it's not surprising that most of the players who developed under Hopman had good volleys. He stressed the attacking style of tennis. Some players, like Mervyn Rose and Rex Hartwig, had better volleys than groundstrokes. These guys moved quickly. They got to the net *fast*. Quickness is what makes a player like Nastase such a good volleyer. Not so much his technical facility for the shot, but the fact that he closes to the net so quickly.

Rod. And Muscles. Everybody talks about his backhand, but his volley on either side is almost as good.

Rod. He worked on it. Rosewall doesn't have a big serve, and figured that with his physique, he was never going to develop one. So he concentrated instead on developing a good volley. He can hit backcourt volleys as accurately as anybody since Sedgman. So even if his serve doesn't overwhelm you, you still have to hit a good, forcing return, otherwise he's going to put a volley deep into the corner and be at your throat for the putaway volley.

Roy. And he doesn't hit the volley very hard —not as hard as Newcombe hits it or as hard as Lew Hoad used to hit it. It's a precise, quick jab. That's all you have to do with the volley: time it well and hit it cleanly. The less arm the better.

Rod. I know I get into trouble when I try to put too much muscle into the volley—especially the backhand volley. The best way to hit it is the way Tony Roche and Emmo do: short, quick, and strong, like a pistol shot.

The Basics of the Volley

The whole point of the volley is to get your strings on the ball the easiest and quickest way possible. You don't have time for a big backswing, and there is no need for a long follow-through. Sometimes, the only thing you have to do to hit a winning volley is to stick the racket in the path of the ball and block it back. Here are the basics.

1. Start in the Proper Ready Position

The waiting position for the volley is essentially the same as the waiting position for groundstrokes: weight forward, feet comfortably spread, free hand cradling the racket near the throat. If there is a difference, it's in the degree of crouching. Since you're closer to the net on volleys, you have to make doubly sure that your weight is forward.

2. Use the Continental Grip

Most volleys are hit near the net, where the ball comes so quickly there usually isn't time to change grips. A grip that works equally well for the forehand and backhand volley alike is the Continental grip, in which the flat top edge of the racket sits in the middle of the "V" between the thumb and index finger.

3. Pivot Shoulders Early

From the ready position, the first thing Rod and Roy do in preparing for the volley is to get their shoulders turned so that they're side-on to the net. Getting the feet side-on helps, too, but frequently there isn't time.

That's why the shoulder turn is so important. Notice in both cases, forehand and backhand, the racket is brought no further back than the back shoulder. The racket head is slightly above the wrist. How high you bring the racket back will depend on the height at which you hope to make contact.

4. Hit the Ball in Front

The further in front you hit the volley, the sharper the angle and usually the better the shot. Advanced players usually open up the racket face a shade, the better to impart underspin. Beginners should simply concentrate on meeting the ball with a squared-up racket face and a firm wrist. The swing is short, with not much follow-through. The racket head does not drop below the wrist. If you have to make contact with the ball below the net, open up the angle of the racket face just a bit, and don't try to do much with the shot.

A FINAL LOOK

Roy. The best way to learn to volley is not to worry in the beginning about "hitting" it and concentrate instead on getting the racket in the path of the ball, and blocking it back. I can't emphasize enough the importance of getting the shoulders turned, especially on the backhand volley. When you're first learning the volley, have somebody toss you some balls as you stand close to the net. Then have someone bounce the ball and hit it to you. Easy! Once you can block back thrown or slowly hit balls, you can gradually work your way to the big time. Be careful where you stand. The best position to be in for volleying is six to eight feet behind the net. Resist the temptation to get closer. That's called "crowding." It's not good because when you're standing that close, you don't have time to react. Another thing: practice volleys with your mates by just hitting the ball before it bounces to one another from the service line. You can do it even in your backyard. It will be hard to control at first, but stay with it until you can keep the ball in play 20 or so times.

THE SERVE

Rod. We could probably spend the better part of a week talking about nothing but the serve. It's the hardest stroke in tennis to learn and, at just about any level of tennis, it's the most important.

Roy. No question about it. If your serve is working well for you, it usually shows up in the rest of your game. You're not worried about losing the serve, and you play with more confidence. Most of the important matches I've lost in my career have been because of my serve, and if I had to do it all over again, I would have probably spent more time developing it, getting it more under control.

Rod. Controlling the serve is everybody's problem. When I played Connors in Las Vegas, I simply couldn't get the first serve in. Once I started getting the serve grooved, I won some games, but it kept coming and going. I couldn't get any consistency.

Roy. Consistency is really what you're looking for on the serve. Some people measure the effectiveness of a server by the number of aces he chalks up in a game. But what good are ten aces in a match if you double-fault as many times? Nobody in tennis serves the ball harder than Colin Dibley, but Colin loses as many points on double faults as he wins points on aces. John Newcombe has a booming serve, too, but he has a very dependable second serve that's almost as hard to deal with as his first serve.

Rod. All we're saying is that unless you get

the bloody thing in, it doesn't matter how hard you hit it. That's why beginners should focus not on hitting the ball hard but on developing a smooth, rhythmic motion.

Roy. Like mine.

Rod. That's a laugh. Emmo has a great serve, but he has what some people describe as a herky-jerky motion.

Roy. Herky-jerky! That sounds like a sandwich. Okay, I tend to wind up a bit on my backswing, a habit I don't recommend. The best service model to follow, I suppose, is Pancho Gonzalez. Now there is a smooth, flowing serve, nothing herky-jerky at all.

Rod. The thing everyone can learn from Pancho is how deliberate he is in his motion. The toss and the backswing are done in almost slow motion; it doesn't even look as if he's swinging hard until the ball comes zinging by you.

Roy. That's what a smooth, rhythmic swing does. You've got enough going for you, with the arm, wrist, and the racket head coming around, that you really don't have to swing hard to get good pace on the ball. But the swing is only half the problem. It's the toss that gets most people in trouble.

Rod. It does me. As soon as I start getting a little tired in a match, the first thing that usually happens is that I don't get the toss quite as high as I should. Usually, it's because I'm rushing it too much.

Roy. Rushing the serve is the biggest mistake players at every level of the game make, particularly after they miss the first serve. With some players it's as if they're so embarrassed about missing the first serve that they want to get the second serve over with as soon as possible. Get out of that habit early. Take your time on both serves, and *think* about what you're doing. That's the one luxury you have on the serve that you don't have on any other stroke: you can control the pace by yourself.

The Basics of the Serve

There are two separate but very much related elements in the serve: the toss and the swing. They work together, but should be learned independently, like learning to play a piano piece by practicing the left hand and right hand individually. Although there are three serves in tennis—the flat, or cannonball; the spin, or slice; and the twist—Rod and Roy teach a single serve to beginners: a flat serve with a slight spin. Here are the mechanics:

1. Use the Continental Grip (see page 62)

Most beginners find it easiest to use an Eastern forehand grip on the serve, but it's better to get accustomed from the start to a Continental grip. It puts a little more spin into the ball which, in turn, gives you more control.

2. Assume the Proper Stance

The important thing about the service position is being relaxed. Rod is standing side-on. His feet are more or less parallel and shoulder width apart. His front foot is pointing slightly outward. He holds the racket and the ball at belt height. In singles, the best place to stand is near the midline; in doubles (see page 135) you should move further toward the sideline.

3. Don't Rush the Toss

The key to a good service toss is: one, taking your time; and two, holding on to the ball until the last second. Rod's tossing arm drops slightly and then starts upward—slowly! The upward movement is straight. The ball is released just as the arm reaches its highest point. He aims the toss so that the ball travels a little more than a racket's length above his outstretched hand, and far enough in front of his body so that if allowed to bounce, it would land about a foot in front of the front foot. Technically, it's not a toss at all. The ball is simply a continuation of the upward arm motion. There should be as little spin as possible. Think soft. Think of the ball as an egg. Soft-boiled.

4. Take a Full Backswing

If you let it happen, the backswing on the serve will take care of itself. The trick is letting the racket drop straight down at the time of the toss. The downward momentum should carry the racket close to the body and back, pendulum style. Once the arm reaches shoulder height, bending the elbow back will drop the racket head down behind the back. That's the so-called back-scratch position. Now your arm is in almost exactly the same position as a baseball player getting set to throw.

5. Hit the Ball at the Highest Possible Point

The serve is best hit at the highest point your arm and racket reach when fully extended. The contact point should be about a foot in front of the body but it won't be unless you've tossed the ball correctly. At this point the racket will just be beginning its downward motion. Some wrist snap is called for at this point. The more advanced you get, the more wrist you'll use. The snapping of the wrist provides the last-second whip of the racket head, and generates most of the pace in the serve.

6. Follow Through on the Opposite Side of the Body

The simple rule on the follow-through: If you're right-handed, the racket comes across your body and finishes up on the left side. If you're a lefty, it's the other way around. Don't be shy about letting the racket come *all* the way down. When Rod serves, his racket sometimes grazes the court surface on the follow-through.

A FINAL LOOK

Rod. The best way to master the serve is to work on it the way my first coach, Charlie Hollis, had me practice it: hitting against a fence. The logic behind this strategy is to master the basic motion before you worry about putting the ball in. The reason so few intermediates serve really well is that as beginners they concentrated too much on getting the ball in and never developed a fundamentally sound serving motion. Strive for rhythm on the stroke. Work on the toss separately. Get to a point where you can throw the ball up to more or less the same place every time. Practice the service swing without the toss. Get a sense of what it feels like to have the racket back and down in the back-scratching position. And be patient. Don't overdo practicing the serve, because it takes a lot out of your arm, but try and work in a certain amount of practice time devoted to the serve alone. The more you work with the serve in the beginning, the easier it's going to be to develop a good one later on.

THE RETURN OF SERVE

Rod. If a magic genie were to give me a choice between having the best serve in tennis or the best return of serve, I'd have to give it a lot of thought.

Roy. That is a tough choice. That's like a doctor telling some of the younger fellows on the tour they have to give up either beer or women.

The older you get, the more important the return of service becomes. The serve may be the most important stroke in singles, but in doubles—which you start to play a lot more as you grow older—the return is *the* most important stroke. In the majority of cases, the return of serve—how weak it is or how strong it is—will determine which side wins the point.

Rod. It's plenty important in singles, too. Some players owe most of the money they've earned in tennis to their great service returns. Rosewall, for one. And Jimmy Connors. Me, too, for that matter. One of the things that makes Connors so tough is that he can hit forcing returns from either side. He attacks almost every serve. I try to do the same thing, but mainly on second serves. When I'm feeling confident, it works.

Roy. Attacking on the service return is the obvious strategy against good players who don't have punishing serves—if you can do it. The big reason Connors was able to run through Rosewall so easily in the 1974 Wimbledon and Forest Hills finals was that Kenny has no working margin on the serve. Most players can't hit out on their returns on both sides, so when Kenny plays, say, Newcombe, he can concentrate on the backhand and pressure Newk with his first volley. Against Connors, though, the returns come back so hard from either side and come in so low that even Kenny, with his great volley, couldn't do anything with them. In those 1974 finals, he was either getting passed or was hitting such weak defensive volleys that Connors had easy putaways on the next shot. It's just a case of one guy's strength being plugged right into another guy's weakness.

Rod. Well, maybe it serves Muscles right. Gives him a dose of his own medicine. Until Connors came along, it was Rosewall's return of service everybody worried about. I've watched matches in which players serving to Rosewall have actually retreated back behind the baseline right after they hit the ball—that's how much they respected Kenny's return.

Roy. That might not have been bad strategy for Rocket in those WCT Finals.

Rod. Emmo had to bring it up, didn't he?

Roy. Bring *what* up?

Rod. The WCT finals in 1972, against Rosewall.

Roy. *I* didn't bring it up. We started talking about Rosewall's return of service . . .

Rod. Now he's bringing it up again: It's bad enough we show the film highlights almost every week at our Tennis Holidays. There I am, ahead 5–4 in the tie-breaker of the final set. I need just two points to win, and I've got two serves coming.

Roy. Nothing to worry about. In like Flynn. Just belt in two great serves.

Rod. Which, of course, is what I did. Two very tough serves, only Kenny's returns were a little tougher. Two boomers—one cross-court, the other down the line. Incredible.

Roy. I'll say. And the interesting thing about both of those returns is what Kenny told me later. He told me he had made his mind up that he was going to go for broke on both returns. That's really the key to being effective on return of service.

Rod. What, being Kenny Rosewall?

Roy. No, having a plan of action. Knowing ahead of time what you want to do with the serve wherever it happens to come. You might be saying to yourself, "Okay, if it comes down the middle to my backhand, I'm just going to get my racket out there and block the ball back." Or, like Ken did against you, you might say, "Okay, I'm going to hit the bloody cover off the ball." It will all depend, of course, on the situation: how well the other guy is serving, how well you're returning, and how the match is going.

Rod. And the plan we recommend for beginners is a very simple one: Get the ball back over the net. The best advice anybody can give on the return of service is not to overdo it. The one thing you don't want to do is to give away a point. Many of the best players, especially the European players, like Nastase and Orantes, rarely go for winners on return of service. They just concentrate on getting the ball back, on putting the pressure back on the server. It works for them. It should work for you.

Roy. Then again, if you can control the return of serve you're in a good position to take the offensive. I relied a lot on my return of service when I was playing tournaments. I varied my strategy according to the server. If he was attacking behind the serve, I would try, mainly, not to give him a return that was easy to volley. I'd keep it low and if I could manage it, I'd chip some angled returns back —something that Rocket does very well off his backhand. If he was staying back, I'd go for a deep return in either corner. One thing I made it a point to avoid was getting into a pattern on my returns. This is a common mistake—even among good players. Without knowing it, you start getting the ball back to the same place. A really good player will recognize this, and go to that spot after every serve.

The Basics of the Return of Serve

The return of service, either forehand or backhand, is nothing more than a normal groundstroke—with one exception. Against good players, the ball is generally coming at you with a good dose of pace and a good dose of spin. The mechanics of the return will depend on how hard, and where, the ball is coming in. On serves hit very hard, the best thing is simply to block the ball back almost as if it were a volley. Just make sure your weight is moving *into* the ball. On balls hit slowly, resist the habit of poking or swiping. Follow all the basic rules for groundstrokes already covered. The fundamentals:

1. Assume the Proper Waiting Position

The best place to await the serve, usually, is about a foot from the place on the court where the singles endline intersects the baseline. This gives you a roughly equal shot at serves hit to either the backhand or forehand side. On the other hand, you should always adjust your position in relation to the serving pattern of your opponent. The ready position is similar to the ready position already covered (see page 51). The grip is midway between the Eastern forehand and backhand.

2. *Pivot Early*

Getting the shoulders turned and the racket back quickly—these two preparatory movements are even more important on the return of service than on regular groundstrokes. Roy uses his front hand to push the racket back. His backswing, however, is shorter than on normal groundstrokes, when there is more time to prepare.

3. Move Into Ball with an Extra Firm Grip

When you're making contact on return of service, you must move your weight into the ball, as Roy is doing in these sequences. He grips the racket extra firmly on contact. A firm grip counteracts the speed or spin of the serve.

4. Adjust Follow-through to Backswing

The length of the follow-through on service returns should correspond with the backswing. Roy's backswing on the backhand is longer than his backswing on the forehand. Hence, he has a longer follow-through on the backhand side.

A FINAL LOOK

Roy. Concentration and confidence are the two keys to successful service returning. Don't weigh yourself down with a lot of technical worries. Against a good server, you don't have the time. Watch the ball carefully. Hit it in front of you with your weight moving forward, and squeeze your grip extra tight. And don't forget about practicing service returns. This is one stroke that hardly anybody in tennis practices enough and yet you hit it almost as often as you hit a serve. Get a friend to serve to both, your backhand and forehand—especially the backhand, since that's where you're going to get served to the most.

THE LOB

Rod. If there's one bit of strategic advice we give out more than any other to the better players who spend time with us at our Tennis Holidays, it's simply this: lob more.

Roy. And more. And more. And more. The lob isn't the sissy shot some intermediate players seem to think it is. And it's not simply a safety-valve shot, something you pull out only when you're scrambling for a ball and want time to get back into position. It's a crucial part of the all-around game. I never realized how crucial until I started playing European clay tournaments in the early 1960s. When I played Rocket in the French Championships in 1962, I was ahead two sets to love but still lost. The reason I lost was that Rod kept crowding the net more and more, and I was too pigheaded to lob. If Rod had been a true friend, he would have told me this *during* the match and not afterward. Anyway, I spent the next twelve months developing a good lob. Without it, I don't think I would have been nearly as successful in the years that followed.

Rod. The lob's been good to me, too. It helped me, for one, in the opening match of the World Cup in 1975, in Hartford, against Dickie Stockton. We were in the tie-breaker of the final set, and it was 6–6. One point either way and the match was either won or lost. Dickie hit a good serve, but I got it back. Shallow but back. He hit a great approach shot and started to close very fast to the net.

The ball was hit to my backhand side, and it would have taken an almost perfect passing shot to get it by him. So I just flicked it over his head. If he'd been standing a little further away from the net, it would have been an easy overhead winner for him, but it just got over his head. He managed to race back and get it, but I was at the net and had a fairly easy backhand volley for the set.

Roy. There is no such thing as a "fairly easy" backhand volley at match point. But I go along with your feeling that the key shot in that rally was the lob. I can think of a lot of matches where a lob proved the difference. Fred Stolle once beat Dennis Ralston in a Davis Cup match with the help of a lob that landed right on the baseline. Some of the fans got on Dennis for not trying for the ball, but Dennis said later that the lob was so well disguised that he knew there was no way in the world, with his knees, he could ever get to it. The only thing he could do was hope that it went out.

Rod. I guess Fred hoped a little harder. But when we're talking about lobs—and I don't want to start sounding like a broken record—we have to start talking again about Muscles.

Roy. No way to avoid it. Muscles doesn't put all that much topspin into his lobs—not like Rocket or Nastase—but he's so quick he has made it an attacking weapon. He also manages to run down balls you think you've hit for winners and to flick them back, high and deep. And all the time you're backpedaling, you're thinking to yourself, "The bloody guy, he's doing it again." You're tempted to let the ball drop, but you know it's going to catch the line, as if the ball had eyes.

Rod. I could have used some of those "eyes" in my Las Vegas match with Connors. I hit two or three lobs early in the match, and they all went out by a foot or so. I hit them a little too hard, and that's a common mistake on the lob.

Roy. Another common mistake is not hitting the ball *high* enough.

Rod. That's for sure. The best advertisement for high lobbing I can think of is Newcombe.

Newcombe hits his lobs so high you get a stiff neck trying to follow the ball. He must have hit dozens of them in our Wimbledon final in 1969, and by the time the fifth set came around, I began to wonder if I would ever be able to look straight ahead again. Manolo Santana was another great lobber. One year at Wimbledon he beat me in five sets and it was the lob that did it. He had me running back on so many points, I just ran out of gas in the final minutes. Santana is such a good-natured guy you wonder why he'd take so much delight wearing you out like that. Both Newk's and Santana's philosophy is that they're going to make sure, first of all, to get the ball over their opponent's head, and then worry about whether or not the ball is going to stay in.

The Basics of the Lob

Except for the topspin lob, which we'll be looking into later on, the lob isn't a very complicated shot. The preparation for the stroke is no different than for any other groundstroke. The swing is similar, too, except that at the last moment you bring the strings under the ball and *lift*. A closer look:

1. Prepare as You Would for Any Groundstroke
Rod and Roy prepare for the lob as they would for a normal backhand or forehand with the appropriate grip. They're facing side-on to the net. The racket is back early. Half the battle of lobbing is keeping the stroke disguised until the last second.

2. *Meet the Ball in Front with an Open Racket*

As with any groundstroke, the best place to make contact with the ball on a lob is in front of the body. The difference between the lob and a normal groundstroke begins to tell just prior to the moment of contact. That's when you open up the racket face and lift upward.

3. *Take a Full Follow-through*

The follow-through is as important on the lob as it is on the forehand or backhand drive. Notice that Rod and Roy are in roughly the same position they'd be in if they were hitting normal groundstrokes, the only difference being that the racket isn't too far in front.

A FINAL LOOK

Roy. The lob is a "touch shot." You pretty much have to develop an instinctive feel for how hard you have to hit it in order to get it over the head of your opponent and still keep it in the court. And a good way to develop this feel is to practice the shot on your own, just standing on the baseline and bouncing the ball yourself, seeing how many you hit close to the baseline on the other side of the court. The key to the shot is the point at which the ball reaches its highest peak. On a still day, or indoors, the ball should reach its highest point directly above the net. If you have wind behind you—and lobbing with the wind at your back is like entering a beer-drinking contest with a full stomach—you'll have to compensate and get the ball higher earlier. Whatever you do, don't just hit the shot blindly. Take your time on the shot. Aim it. Keep the wrist firm. And don't forget to practice it. Fifteen minutes or so, every once in a while, of bouncing balls and practicing lobs on your own will do wonders.

THE OVERHEAD

Rod. There isn't a whole lot you can say about the overhead except that it is strictly an offensive shot that requires a lot of confidence, a lot of decisiveness, and a lot of practice. Probably the best advice I can give anybody on the stroke is advice my old coach Charlie Hollis first gave me. "Don't mess with the smash, Rodney," he used to say. "Kill it!"

Roy. There's nothing wrong with that advice. There have been a number of top players—John Bromwich, for one—who occasionally lost big matches because they couldn't put away the smash. Once your opponent knows you don't have a good smash, he's probably going to lob you to death—unless he happens to be a very gentle person like myself. I won't lob you to *death*, but I will make you suffer a little.

Rod. Not being able to put the overhead away means giving your opponent a second or third chance. You can't do that when you're at the net. Sooner or later, he's going to get it by you. The smash, by the way, is one stroke for which being tall is a big help in tennis. It's one of the reasons Pancho Gonzalez was so effective with his smash. Those extra few inches gave him that much better an angle. Of course, there have been great smashers who weren't that tall. Lew Hoad is about my size, but he had a fearful overhead. He timed it very well and always hit it very hard—so hard you were amazed the ball didn't put a hole in the court.

Roy. Hoad had loads of confidence, and that's what you need more than anything else on the overhead. More than any other stroke, the overhead is the one you have to think *positively* about. The minute you get a little tentative or unsure of yourself on the overhead, you might as well not hit it. Sometimes you have a lot of time to think about hitting, and this can be either good or bad depending upon who you are and how well you're playing. If things aren't going well for you and your opponent puts up a lob a mile high, you'd be surprised at all the things that pop into your head. You start thinking to yourself, "Oh, no, am I going to miss this?" And you do. Then you get another lob and you figure to make up for it, so you hit it with all your might and you miss again. Now you really feel like jumping off a bridge. And you keep

doing that until you learn to relax on the stroke, to wait until the precise moment and just to pick it off, clean and simple.

Rod. The sort of physical shape you're in is also going to have a lot to do with how well you hit the overhead, especially late in the match. Half the problem with the stroke is getting back under it quickly enough. You don't have much time, and if you take it too easy, you have to hit the ball when it's behind you, and it's hard to control it. When I start missing overheads late in the match, you can be sure I'm running out of gas. It's a problem a lot of players run into in the fifth set. I can't tell you how many times I've watched Rosewall lob an opponent—me included—silly in the fifth set. Muscles loves to do it when it's a very hot day and there's a bright sun. You keep looking up into that sun and you start seeing two or three balls up there and you don't know which one to hit.

Roy. But if you're hitting it well, a good overhead smash does wonders for your morale. I don't think there's a more satisfying experience in tennis than to pick the ball out of the air and smash it down—wham! You can get rid of a lot of aggression that way, and I especially enjoy it when I'm doing it against certain red-headed, slightly-bow-legged Australians.

The Basics of the Overhead

Getting the racket back, getting the body turned early, and moving under the ball before it goes over your head—these are the essential points to bear in mind about the overhead. The backswing is best thought of as a modified service motion. Here are the basics:

1. Use the Continental Grip (see page 62)

Because the swing approximates the serve, the Continental grip works best for the overhead.

2. Turn Side-on to Net

Overheads should never be hit—except in emergencies—with the body facing the net. Here, Rod, gets his body side-on and takes the racket back in an abbreviated service swing.

3. Bring the Racket Back with a Modified Service Motion

Nothing fancy here. Just get the racket back in the same position you'd bring it to if you were serving.

4. Position Yourself Under the Ball

Learning how to judge the flight of a lob is a little like learning how to judge a high pop-up in baseball. Judgment comes from practice. Rod is now standing in the ideal place to be standing under a lob. If he let the ball drop, it would hit him square in the forehead. Like most pros, he uses his free hand to track the ball and to keep his balance.

5. Make Contact as High as Possible

A repeat performance of the serve: making contact with the ball at the uppermost point of the swing, slightly in front of the body. Notice that Rod's wrist snaps into the ball at the last possible second. His grip is extra firm. He also avoids a common error: letting his head drop down before contact.

6. Follow Through Out and Down

There is a tendency when hitting the overhead to drag the racket head down too sharply. This usually results in the ball slamming into the net. Rod's follow-through on the overhead is as long as possible, with the racket ending up low and on the other side of the body.

7. Let High Deep Lobs Bounce First

On balls hit very high and relatively deep, it is a good practice to let the ball bounce first before you try to hit them. The same general techniques apply on overheads hit on one bounce that apply to overheads hit on the fly. The important thing is to make contact with the ball before it drops too low after the bounce.

A FINAL LOOK

Rod. The big problem with learning the overhead is getting somebody to hit you lobs so you can practice it. It's not a convenient stroke to practice since the ball rarely stays in play after you've hit the stroke—at least it shouldn't if you're hitting it well. Ball machines are a great help for an overhead practice session, but don't start slamming away until your arm is good and warm. One of the ways I used to practice the overhead when I was younger was to stand at the net and pretend I was being lobbed, skipping back as quickly as I could to different parts of the court. As with any stroke, concentrate in the beginning on developing a nice, rhythmic swing. Don't swing hard; just try to make solid contact. Once you've got the timing down a little, then you can begin to put a little more mustard into it. You can also start experimenting with changing the direction of the ball, an even better strategy than hitting hard. The main reason Kenny Rosewall's overhead is so effective isn't that he hits the ball hard but that he waits until the last second and puts the ball wherever he wants. He doesn't even move his feet; he just turns his shoulders one way or the other.

C H A P T E R

3

Developing the Not-So-Basic Shots

Nobody (well, almost nobody) stays a beginner at tennis forever. Eventually you reach a point at which you are no longer astonished by the fact that the balls you hit actually clear the net, land within the confines of the opposite court and, on occasion, accomplish this miraculous journey with a surprising amount of pace. No longer consumed by the mere idea of getting the ball over the net, you now concentrate on hitting the ball to specific areas on the court. You swing harder. You move with more confidence. You begin telling yourself that had you only started playing at an earlier age, a shot at Wimbledon would not be out of the question. You still experience sporadic periods of ineptitude, of course, but you take it in stride. Sometimes. In the meantime, you boldly venture forward into unexplored areas. You think you're nearing the end. Actually, you've only begun.

Rod. One of the best things about tennis—and the one thing that differentiates it from a lot of sports—is that you can play the sort of game that's more or less tailored to your age, your build, your ability, and your temperament. But at whatever level—or intensity—you play it, it helps to have a variety of techniques. Some people develop their technique only to the point where they can beat their regular partners. Once they start winning, they stop thinking about developing. I think this is a mistake.

Roy. I agree. There's a big difference between winning and developing. We run into some players at our Tennis Holidays who have been thinking about one thing only since they started playing: winning. We'll find a fellow or girl who has a murderous serve and nothing else except perhaps a better-than-average forehand. Now you can win a lot of matches with this sort of game—at least in singles—but you're limited as to what you can do with it. It doesn't do you much good in doubles. It's useless in mixed doubles. Rather than see you develop this kind of game, we think you're much better off developing a reasonably sound all-around game. By this we mean a game in which you can hit most of the shots in tennis with a reasonable amount of control.

Rod. It's not as hard as you may think to develop the sort of game Emmo is talking about. You simply have to put your mind to it. I've seen intermediate players who can't play the net. I ask them why, they tell me they can't volley. That's nonsense. If you can hit groundstrokes, you can volley. The volley is actually an easier stroke to hit. What this person is really telling me is that he doesn't want to take the time to develop a volley. Fine, if that's the way he wants to approach the game, but let's get our reasons straight. There isn't a stroke in tennis that's too difficult for the average player to develop, if you put your mind to it. You do it gradually. If you want to hit better backhand volleys, for instance, practice the stroke more in your pre-match hit-ups. Go to net more, even if you make errors and lose the point. It's the only way you're going to learn and develop. If you're concerned only about winning, of course, you can't do this. That's why some super-competitive athletes never develop into good tennis players. They don't have the patience.

Roy. Time and patience—you need both to build the sort of all-around tennis game that will give you the most enjoyment. You can't expect to hit winners off a new stroke the first or second time you use it in a match, so don't give up on it. Take a good look at some of the more advanced techniques we'll be present-ing in this chapter. Sample them. Live with them for a while. Experiment. The price is right.

GETTING SPIN TO WORK FOR YOU

Rod. A good way to begin our look into ad-vanced techniques is to talk about spin and where it fits into the scheme of things in ten-nis. And since Emmo is an expert in scientific matters—after all, *Playboy* runs plenty of sci-ence articles—I'm going to let him start.

Roy. It all comes down to physics, pure and simple. The way a ball is spinning as it travels through the air will have an effect on the way it interacts with air pressure, and this interaction, in turn, is going to affect both how fast it travels and how far it travels. Spin is also going to affect what the ball does when it bounces.

Rod. There are three types of spin we're concerned with in tennis: overspin, under-spin, and *almost no* spin. Overspin is usually referred to as "topspin." The ball is rotating forward as it travels. Underspin is usually re-ferred to as "slice." The ball is rotating back-ward as it travels. Any ball traveling with no spin at all is referred to as a "flat" ball. It's rare, though, that a ball has no spin at all, so "flat" is used to describe any ball with a small amount of spin. (There's another type of spin—sidespin—but it doesn't have much relevance in tennis, so we won't talk about it.)

Roy. In advanced tennis, spin is synonymous with control. On a flat ball, the momentum of the racket is transferred *directly* to the ball. Spin changes that relationship. If a ball is spinning forward—that is, with topspin—it will interact with air pressure in a way that will force the ball down sooner than it would if the same ball was hit with the same power and with no spin, or with underspin. On the other hand, a ball hit with underspin will tend to float more. So what it comes down to is this: with topspin, you can hit the ball harder and still keep it in the court; with underspin, you can get depth without having to hit the ball hard.

Rod. Players who use a lot of spin in their games are generally referred to as spin artists. People think of players like Tony Roche and myself as spin players, but we rely mostly on topspin, not slice. Topspin happens to suit the way I like to play tennis: aggres-sively. My game has always been based on attack, on hitting "out." The only way you can hit hard and still have some control is to "top" the ball. I shouldn't say "only" way; Jimmy Connors hits the ball hard and fairly flat. He can do it because he times the ball well and keeps the racket head in that flat hitting plane longer than most players. The ball stays on the racket a little longer, and that's what gives him the control. The true spin artists of tennis are Europeans and South Americans—players like Borg, Vilas or Santana. The reason you see more spin among these players is that most of them grew up playing on clay, whereas most of the Ameri-cans or Australians grew up playing on either grass or cement. On clay, power alone isn't enough, so the better players use a mix-ture of spin to keep their opponents off bal-ance. Some of them—particularly Santana— can drive you nuts because you never get the same ball twice in a row and it's impossible to develop a playing rhythm.

Roy. Of course, it's not easy to hit spin shots consistently and not make your share of errors. The minute you start putting spin into your shots, the more you increase your mar-gin for error—unless you develop the neces-sary touch. My feeling about spin shots is that you should know how to hit them but you shouldn't use spin excessively. Too many younger players today are getting carried

away with topspin. It's good to use on passing shots, but I don't recommend a steady diet of topspin for baseline-to-baseline drives. For one thing, it's hard to generate depth with baseline drives hit with topspin, and if you're up against a good player, he can take a short ball and put away the return. Then, too, the ball is kicking up when it bounces, and this gives your opponent plenty of time to hit it back. Finally, it takes a lot out of you, pounding topspin forehand after topspin forehand. As for underspin, a little bit of it on volleys helps you control them, and it works well on approach shots. You have a little more time to get into the net behind a slice approach shot, and because the bounce isn't too high on a slice shot, your opponent has a tougher job hitting a passing shot.

The Basics of Spin

The spin on the ball once it leaves the racket is determined by the relationship of the racket head to the ball upon contact and the racket head movement just after contact. In the last chapter, we went over flat groundstrokes. Here are the hitting fundamentals for the basic spin shots of tennis.

The Slice or Underspin Forehand

Most of the principles that apply to the flat forehand apply to forehands hit with spin. The grip is the same, the ready position is the same, and the basic footwork and body position are the same. Here are the differences:

1. Take the Racket Back Higher

Since you're swinging down and through the ball on a slice forehand, it stands to reason that the stroke will start high and finish low. The general rule of thumb is to raise the racket head higher than the flight path of the approaching ball.

2. Contact the Ball at an Angle

Roy meets the ball on a slice forehand about the same place he does on the flat forehand. The difference is the angle of the racket head on contact. Notice it is open, at about a 45° angle. This is what imparts the backspin. Roy's body weight is moving into the ball. His wrist is firm, but not like a vise. He tries to "stay with" the shot by keeping the ball on the strings as long as possible.

3. Take a Full Follow-through

There is a tendency on the slice forehand to abbreviate the follow-through. Roy has made contact with the ball at a downward angle. He lets the racket head flow down and through the ball so that he is in a lower finishing position than he would have been in had he hit the ball flat.

A FINAL LOOK

Roy. The slice forehand is a useful stroke, but it doesn't take the place of a flat forehand or a topspin forehand. The problem with it is that it's not an attacking stroke, and if you can't attack with your forehand, your game isn't going to have much firepower. Another problem is that the slice forehand doesn't work very well as a passing shot: it simply doesn't get over the net fast enough. On the other hand, it's good to use on approach and comes in handy, too, on return of service—particularly against someone who's got a high kicking serve. What you want to remember when you hit the stroke is not to cut it short. Stay with the ball as long as you can and give the follow-through the full treatment.

The Slice Backhand

The mechanics of the slice backhand are roughly similar to the mechanics of the slice forehand. Starting high and meeting the ball with an angled racket face are the keys. The other elements—ready position, side-on body position, follow-through, etc.—retain their importance. Here are the main things to remember.

1. Open Up the Racket Head on the Backswing

Since the racket head is going to be angled when Roy contacts the ball on the slice backhand, he opens up the angle of the racket face slightly on the backswing. Notice, too, that he brings the racket back a little more behind his body. This is a personal technique used by some players to give the racket head more "whip" when it comes around.

2. Meet the Ball in Front with the Full Swing

The best place to make contact with the slice backhand is about a half-foot or so in front of the front foot. Notice Roy's racket stays slightly open at impact. His wrist remains locked.

3. Don't Short-Circuit the Follow-through

The follow-through for the slice backhand is roughly as high as that of the topspin backhand—the difference is the swing goes down and then up. Keep the follow-through long and flowing.

A FINAL LOOK

Roy. Most beginners and intermediates hit slice backhands without really being aware of it, but they don't use the stroke to best advantage. A little bit of underspin is useful for the backhand because you can cut down just a bit on the swing and still get distance with it. Too much underspin, though, robs the stroke of power. As in the case of the forehand, use the slice backhand mainly for approach shots and for defensive returns of service. And keep in mind that it's a full stroke, not a poke. The reason so many of the beginners' underspin backhands sail way beyond the baseline is that the strings do not stay on the balls long enough to generate control.

The Topspin Forehand

There are essentially two ways to generate topspin on groundstrokes. One way is to roll the wrist sharply over the ball at the moment of contact. That's the way most of the topspin artists in the professional game do it. It's also the hard way. An easier and more dependable way—although it doesn't generate quite the same degree of spin—is to go from low to high on the stroke, letting the natural motion of the stroke and not the last-minute turn of the wrist set the spin in motion. As with the slice shots, the basic elements—grip, preparatory movements, etc.—remain the same as for all groundstrokes. Here are the differences.

1. Start the Backswing Lower

Roy prepares for a topspin forehand as he would any groundstroke, with one major difference. The racket head during the looped backswing drops *below* the flight path of the approaching ball.

2. Tilt the Leading Edge of the Racket

Roy makes contact with the ball on line with the front hip, only this time the leading edge of the racket is slanted towards the net. This slightly tilted angle is what enables the racket strings to brush over the ball.

3. Don't Come Off the Ball Too Soon

The professional players who hit a lot of topspin shots tend to whip their rackets over the ball, as if they were cracking a bullwhip. This is hard to do for most players and tough on the arm for everybody. Better to do as Roy does here: take a long, flowing follow-through, as if the ball were being hit flat.

A FINAL LOOK

Roy. I like to see intermediate players hit their forehands with some, but not an excessive amount, of topspin. As we said earlier, it's a more versatile shot than the strictly flat or slice forehand. It takes time in the beginning to get used to hitting "over" the ball, so you should do it in stages. In the beginning, just concentrate on getting the racket head below the flight of the ball. Once you've got that down, then you can start angling the racket face a little toward the net. At first, you'll probably discover most of the balls going into the net, but if you keep at it, eventually you'll be able to brush over the ball and get it to clear the net. Don't cheat on the follow-through, the biggest mistake nearly everyone makes on topspin shots is trying to imitate Rod Laver and Tony Roche by coming off the ball too soon. Keep the body low, even as the racket is going out and up.

The Topspin Backhand

Most players find the topspin backhand more difficult to master than the topspin forehand, and with good reason. It's a more difficult stroke to time, and there's a greater need for wrist movement. Early preparation is essential on this stroke, as is the high follow-through. The key elements in the stroke are:

1. Prepare Early With the Racket Head Low

You need more time to set up for the topspin forehand than for any other groundstroke, so getting side-on and getting the racket back early assume double importance. Roy is in perfect position here for the stroke: The racket is cocked back alongside his trailing hip and is below the ball's flight path, his elbow is tucked into his body, and his arm is comfortably extended.

2. Meet the Ball in Front

Contact point for the topspin backhand is about a foot in front of the leading hip. Notice the angle of the racket face. If it were more open the ball would sail beyond the baseline.

3. *Roll the Wrist over the Ball Slightly*

Rod uses excessive wrist motion on his top-spin backhand, but for most players a modest amount of wrist play over the ball is more than enough. You can tell if you're hitting over the ball by the sound. It's more a brushing sound than a *thwock!*

4. *Follow Through High*

There is no way to overemphasize the importance of a high follow-through on the top-spin backhand. Finishing high completes the low-to-high sequence that imparts the characteristic spin. Don't open up the body too soon. Notice that even while Roy's racket is high, his shoulders are still facing the sideline and his knees are still bent.

A FINAL LOOK

Rod. Most tennis players find the topspin backhand a difficult shot to master, but to me it came fairly naturally. The big reason, I guess, is that right from the beginning of my tennis I was taught to hit the backhand all three ways, and since I figured that with my size I was going to have to do something to match the power of the bigger guys, I concentrated on topspin more than the others. If you're hitting a slice backhand now and want to get more topspin into the stroke, take a fairly gradual approach. Concentrate first on hitting the ball flat, making sure the racket head is moving *through* the ball. Once you can hit the ball flat with a reasonable amount of consistency, then you can start hitting over the ball a little more. You can do this either by lowering the racket head on the backswing or by rolling the wrist over the ball the way I do—whichever comes easier for you. The earlier you meet the ball on the topspin backhand, the better. Don't make the mistake of trying to put topspin into balls that are bouncing low. We all have trouble with those low balls.

It's not that easy to develop a good topspin

backhand, but it can make a major difference in your game. Where it comes in the handy is when you want to put away a ball that's bouncing in the forecourt. If you can't hit with topspin, you can't hit the ball too hard, which means you've got to aim fairly close to the line. Topspin, though, gives you that added measure of control. You may not be able to put the ball exactly where you want it, but you know the ball is going to travel and is going to stay in the court, and even if you hit right to the other player, he's still going to have his hands full trying to get it back.

THE DIFFICULT VOLLEYS

Rod. In the last chapter we spoke about volleys as if there were only one person on the court hitting the ball, only one person trying to win. But if I'm playing Emmo, and I see him charging the net, I'll be hanged if I'm going to give him a ball that he can volley too easily. No sir. He's going to have to sweat nickels to hit it.

Roy. Now, there's a mate for you. But I'm not too worried. One thing you learn quickly if you're going to play aggressive tennis is that you have to hit volleys at every height and every angle. A good volleyer should be able to deal with high volleys, low volleys, in-between volleys, and, maybe once in a while, a behind-the-back volley.

Rod. The behind-the-back volley can wait, but drilling's the key to the other shots. Intermediate players usually don't spend enough time in practice or the warm-up on low or high volleys. These players look terrific on balls that come nicely wrapped, about shoulder high. But comes a match, and they start getting shots drilled at them from every angle, they're helpless.

Roy. Yet difficult volleys aren't always as difficult as they look. The main thing is to play the ball—not let it play you. If it's a low volley, you keep your eyes in line with the ball, getting down as low as you can. You concentrate extra hard. Block the ball back with a very firm wrist, and if you get the ball back, don't stand there congratulating yourself—get ready for the next shot.

Rod. If you want to, of course, you can make a difficult volley look even more difficult than it is. The guy that comes to my mind is Freddie Huber, an Austrian who used to be known as the "Danny Kaye of tennis." Huber didn't just lunge for volleys. He would dive flat out and usually wound up on the ground. He did it for effect, but the crowds used to eat it up. I sometimes wonder how Huber would have fared if he'd have played on the concrete courts of California.

Roy. Not too well. But the best example to follow, again, is Rosewall, especially on the low volleys. It's that balance and quickness again. Roche plays the stroke well. He doesn't try to do too much with it—just gets it back as deep as he can.

Rod. As far as high volleys go, an ugly fellow by the name of Roy Emerson has as good a high backhand volley as anybody.

Roy. I worked at it. The main thing is to get the shoulder around early and to meet the ball in front with a very firm wrist.

Rod. And don't be timid when you hit it.

Roy. No indeed. Think John Wayne.

The Basics of the Low Volley

To volley a ball that has dropped below the top of the net, you have to open up the racket head slightly. You have to do something else, too: bend your knees and get about as low as you can bend. The basic points to remember on the low volley are:

1. Get Your Body Low

Just sticking the racket head down isn't going to get the job done on the low volley. As both Rod and Roy demonstrate, the knees must bend and the body lower so that the eyes stay on line with the ball as much as possible.

2. Open Up the Racket Face

The racket face is always slightly open on the low volley. The degree of openness will depend on how far below the top of the net you make contact. The lower the ball, the more open the racket face.

3. Keep the Follow-through Short

The main thing to think about after you've hit the low volley is to get back to your normal ready position. Rod is already there, set for the return. Roy will bring his back foot up quickly and pivot.

A FINAL LOOK

Rod. The low volley isn't as difficult a shot as it might sometimes look. If you develop the habit early of getting your entire body down instead of just the racket, and if you concentrate on simply meeting the ball with a firm grip and a slightly open racket face, the stroke should take care of itself. A good way to practice this stroke is to go through the serving motion, without the ball, follow the serve to the net, and then, at the service line, dip low to hit an imaginary low volley. Do it on both the forehand and the backhand. Above all, remember that the low volley is a *defensive* shot. Most of the errors that occur on the stroke occur because a player tries to do too much with it.

The Basics of the High Volley

On the forehand side, the high volley is not generally a problem. The main thing is to meet the ball early and not chop down on it. Otherwise the principles of volleying already covered on page 61 cover the stroke nicely. The backhand volley, though, is a different story. Many players find this stroke the most difficult in tennis. Women in particular seem to have trouble generating power with it. There are no special secrets to hitting this stroke. It's more a question of following the basic volleying principles already covered, but with special emphasis on pivoting early and hitting the ball in front. Here are the basics:

1. Turn Your Shoulder Early

As with all volleys, getting the shoulders turned as soon as possible—even before you move your feet—will increase your chances of hitting a successful shot.

2. Keep the Backswing Short

A short backswing is especially crucial on the backhand volley, mainly because hitting the ball in front is your main priority. Notice how Roy uses his free hand to anchor the racket. The racket does not go beyond his back shoulder.

3. Meet the Ball in Front with a Firm Wrist

On both forehand and backhand high volleys, you want to hit the ball well beyond the leading shoulder. This is particularly true of the backhand volley. Your wrist stays firm. Your eyes never leave the ball.

A FINAL LOOK

Roy. Many players, especially women, find the high volley a very difficult stroke. The main reason is that they don't appreciate the importance of getting the shoulders turned quickly. Once the ball gets behind you on the high-volley, you might as well forget about it. A good way to practice the stroke is to have somebody hit balls to you and to start with the racket already back in the hitting position. Meet the ball early and with a firm wrist! Then, once you can hit the ball consistently with the racket back, start from the ready position.

One final thought about difficult volleys in general. Don't give up on them. So many of the winning volleys that I've hit in my career were nothing more than desperation shots. I just threw my body at the ball with the racket straight out. I saw Stan Smith win the crucial game of a Wimbledon final with just that sort of a desperation shot. The ball hit the wood and dribbled over the net for a winner. Some people called it a lucky shot but I've always figured that Smith deserved credit for making the lunge.

THE HALF-VOLLEY

Rod. The half-volley is the judo shot of tennis—the shot you hit in self-defense. Emmo follows his serve to the net, and I hit a low return that bounces right at his feet. The ball is too low to volley, but there's no way Emmo can stop and hit a regular groundstroke. So, he has to half-volley it: get his racket almost on the ground and make contact with the ball as soon as it bounces.

Roy. It's not an easy stroke, but if you're going to play the serve-and-volley game, you'd better learn how to hit it. It's also a very good stroke to have in doubles. If you're up against first-class opponents, they're going to be hitting at your feet all day. One of the things I've always admired about Bob Hewitt's game was his ability to scoop up those low shots and get them over the net. Hewitt is one of the few guys who can sometimes make the half-volley an offensive shot. He hits it so much better than anyone expects that it has a big surprise factor.

Rod. Rosewall's half-volley is pretty to watch, too.

Roy. And what makes his half-volley so good is his body control. He can be moving in full stride up to the net and can still keep his balance as he gets down low to meet the ball that's bouncing at his shoetops. Rosewall's size helps. The half volley is one stroke in tennis for which being small has its advantages. It's usually easier for a small player to get low than a tall player—assuming, of course, the small player has good balance. A couple of tall players I can think of—Pancho Gonzalez for one—hit the half-volley very well because they could move so gracefully.

Rod. The main reason Gonzalez's half-volley was so good, particularly when he was playing serve and volley, was that even after hitting a big serve he never lost his balance. You'd rap a good return right at his feet and you figured he could never hit it, but he would stop quickly, dip down, make contact, and sometimes end up hitting a winner with it. The worst part when you were playing him was how easy he made it seem. I guess boxers must feel that way when they rap the other guy with their Sunday punch and the guy looks back and just smiles.

Roy. Another thing worth remembering on the half-volley is that it helps to be able to hit it from the baseline. Lots of times you're in a situation at the baseline where the ball is going to be bouncing either on or very near the line. A volley from that deep is hardly ever a percentage shot, but you see you're not going to be able to position yourself quickly enough to hit a groundstroke. No problem. If you can hit the half-volley well enough, you can return a deep shot like that fairly regularly.

Rod. But only if you work on it. Hardly anybody practices the half-volley enough, and hardly anybody hits even a few of them during the warm-up. True, it's not a shot you go out of your way to hit, but if you can convert the shot the few times in a match when you have no choice but to hit it, you're going to save some points, and I don't care who you are, on some days a couple of points can mean the difference between winning and losing the match.

The Basics of the Half-Volley

There is no time to prepare for the half-volley (if there were, you wouldn't choose to hit it), and there's nothing in the way of a follow-through. The main thing is to get the body turned early and get down as low as possible for the ball. The basics:

1. Pivot Early

Regardless of where you are on the court, your first reaction, when the ball looks as if it's going to land around your shoetops is to turn the shoulders and get the racket back. Sound familiar?

2. Bend Your Body Low

The lower the better. Notice that Rod has moved his body into the front foot.

3. Keep the Racket Head Above Your Wrist

By keeping the racket head above the wrist you pretty much force yourself to get down low for the ball, not to mention the extra dimension of control it gives you over the racket.

4. Stroke Through the Ball and Follow Through

Rod avoids the common mistake on the half-volley of stopping the racket right after

contact. He keeps the ball on the strings as long as possible, and has followed through on the stroke to give the ball direction.

A FINAL LOOK

Roy. The half-volley is no different from any other stroke in tennis. The only way to master it is to practice it. The best way to practice it is to combine half-volley shots with your regular baseline strokes during baseline rallies. Hit your normal baseline strokes, but every once in a while move in on the ball and pick it off the ground as soon as it bounces.

Another way of developing the stroke is to start your practice rallies with it. Nothing to it. You simply drop the ball, bend, and stroke it as soon as it bounces. Once you get to a point where you can place the half-volley with reasonable consistency, you can start doing a little more with it in match play, but keep in mind it's a defensive shot. If you can avoid losing the point on the half-volley, you'll have more than done the job.

ADVANCED SERVING

Rod. Here we are talking about the serve again.

Roy. Why not? By now, if everybody has followed our earlier instructions, we've got

thousands of Pancho Gonzalezes out there with perfect serving form. From here on it's a question of what you do with the serve now that you've learned it.

Rod. Let's talk first about what you *don't* do: What you don't do is wallop your first serve in like thunder and then, if you miss it, hit a meager little second serve that wouldn't frighten a baby rabbit. This sort of serving philosophy is bad enough in singles, but it's murder in doubles. It puts your partner at the net in the not very pleasant position of having either to surrender his position there or risk having his head knocked off.

Roy. I'll surrender. And let me add this. If you can't get your first serve in at least 75 percent of the time, you're probably serving too hard. It's as simple as that. Okay, your second serve is weak, and you figure you're going to lose the point anyway on the second serve, so why not go for all the marbles on the first. Well, I say develop a second serve. Not a bomb, or a bullet. Just a medium-paced serve that has some spin on it and lands fairly deep.

Rod. The second serve is crucial. If you can depend on your second serve, it takes that much pressure off your first serve. One of the big reasons Newcombe's serve is so well respected, as we said earlier, is that his second serve is almost as tough to handle as some players' first serve. He has so much confidence in both of his bloody serves, he simply cranks up and plows into it. When he's on, he doesn't worry about whether or not he's going to get it in—only where he wants it to go.

Roy. The secret of a good, dependable serve is spin. The only way a flat serve can give anybody any trouble is if it's hit hard. Good and hard. But on a second serve, you can't take the chance of hitting the ball too hard. Very few of the pros do it. Hardly anybody I can think of serves the cannonball on his second serve. With spin, though, you can hit the ball reasonably hard and still control it. You can also aim the ball a little higher over the net and still be fairly certain the ball will not go beyond the service line.

Rod. And if you're really feeling adventurous, you can experiment a bit with the twist serve. That's the one where you bend your body into the shape of a pretzel so that you can give the ball the sort of spin that makes the ball do what it's supposed to do on this serve. And what it does is come over the net with a very high loop, drop sharply, and then kick away from the receiver. If you can hit this serve, it's a very dependable serve and a difficult one for most players to return. It's a good serve for doubles too, because you have more time to get in behind it. Newcombe uses the twist on his second serve and so did Tom Gorman, before he hurt his back.

Roy. Which is the problem with the twist serve. It's rough on your body. Because you're tossing the ball a little behind you, you have to bend your back well around in order to hit the ball. Unless you're very limber to begin with or have a strong back, we don't recommend the twist serve. A good second serve is one thing; a week in traction is another.

The Basics of Serving with Spin

The Slice Serve

Putting spin into the serve doesn't require too much of a deviation from the techniques already covered on the basic serve. (The exception is the American twist serve, which we'll get to in a minute.) A slight change in the grip and the toss is generally enough to let you slice across the ball without making severe changes in the swing. If you're right-handed, a normal spin, or slice, serve will tend to curve to the receiver's right when it bounces, regardless of whether he is standing in the deuce or ad court. The serve is effective when aimed at the backhand side. It forces the returner to hit from a cramped position. The mechanics:

1. Use the Continental Grip

The Continental grip puts the wrist in a better position to generate spin on contact.

2. Don't Telegraph the Toss

The toss for the slice serve should be the same as the toss for the flat serve. You generate the slice with wrist action and follow-through. (Note: When you are first developing a slice serve it might be easier to toss the ball slightly to the right, for righties—left for lefties. Eventually, though, you should try to disguise the serving intention as much as possible.)

3. Contact the Ball at a Slight Angle

The racket is not absolutely flat on contact the way it is for the flat serve. The angle, however, is not too severe and requires a fairly sharp turn of the wrist. The follow-through is across the ball and not out through the ball as in the flat serve. Remember to keep your eye on the ball, to let the weight flow naturally forward, and to finish up with a full follow-through on the opposite side of the body.

The Twist Serve

The key to the twist serve is the toss. At its highest point, the ball is actually behind you. Having tossed it there, the next problem is hitting it—an impossibility unless you not only let the racket drop down and back and bend your back back at a sharp angle as well. The key points:

1. Use the Proper Toss

The toss for the twist serve is crucial. The ball should be thrown up in line with the shoulder opposite your hitting arm and just a shade behind you.

2. Bend Your Body Well Back

Being a contortionist helps on this serve. Notice how low the racket head is on Rod's backswing.

3. Move Your Weight into the Ball on Contact

Since the ball is tossed behind the body, getting the weight moving forward into the ball presents special problems. More's the necessity for that extreme bend as shown in the previous photo.

A FINAL LOOK

Rod. The first few times you try any spin serve, you may think the ball is going to land in the wrong court and you may want to make adjustments with your wrist. Don't. Remember, you're not hitting the ball flat; you're coming across it. The racket may be going one way, but the ball will be going another. Don't worry in the beginning about hitting it hard. If you're having trouble with it, practice the toss by itself, then try it again. But don't let yourself get discouraged. Once you've learned to hit the serve with spin, you'll find it much easier to control than the flat serve. That control will give you added confidence and make your first serve all the more dangerous.

THE DROP SHOT

Rod. I think Emmo should talk about the drop shot because it has special meaning to him. It might have cost him a Wimbledon championship.

Roy. Well, we've already talked about it so why dredge up all the sordid details? I was leading Owen Davidson when he hit a very good drop shot that I ran like hell to get to and wound up banging my shoulder into the umpire's stand. Just thinking about drop shots gives me a pain in the shoulder.

Rod. Okay, we'll make it brief. The drop shot is a touch shot that's harder to develop than it looks. It works much better on clay or grass than it does on a hard surface because it doesn't bounce as high. When it's hit well, the ball will clear the net with very little pace and land very short with almost no bounce or else with backspin. I've seen Santana hit drop shots that have actually bounced back over the net. That's how much backspin he puts on the ball. Most of the players with the best drop shots are Europeans—guys like Santana, Pietrangeli, and Nastase, who've grown up on clay, although Rosewall uses the stroke and so does Newcombe, on occasion.

Roy. When you hit the stroke is almost as important as how you hit it. If you can disguise the shot well, and if you're up against a player who doesn't move too well and doesn't like to come to net, it can be an effective weapon from the baseline. But it's a hard shot to hit from there. The best time to hit the drop shot is when you're near the service line and your opponent is deep in his court or retreating.

Rod. It's not a shot to try when you don't enjoy a positional advantage. A common mistake among club players who like to use the drop shot is that they try it in situations in which only a perfect drop shot is going to win the point for them. You want to hit the ball so that it clears the net by a reasonably safe margin, which means your opponent has to be a long way from it.

Roy. And once you've hit it, don't just stand there waiting to see if the other guy is going to be able to run it down. The usual answer to a drop shot, assuming you can get to it, is another drop shot, so the best place to be is close to the net, where you can hit a volley winner on any short, high ball.

The Basics of the Drop Shot

The drop shot is a "touch" shot. Much of its success lies in how cleverly you disguise it. The rest is finding the happy medium between what will get the ball over the net and still land shallow enough to keep your opponent from running it down. The key points to remember are:

1. Prepare as You Would for Any Groundstroke

Rod and Roy prepare for the drop shot just as if they were going to hit a normal groundstroke. Neither one telegraphs it by angling the racket face.

2. Angle the Racket Face on Contact

The racket face on the drop shot is even more "open" than on the slice. This is one shot in which wrist action is encouraged—not much; just a quick chop-like flick. This chopping motion, coupled with the open angle, gives the ball its characteristic backspin.

3. Keep the Follow-through Simple

Neither follow-through nor weight transfer is crucial on the drop shot. A medium follow-through is enough. What *is* important, though, is to be moving forward as soon as you've hit the stroke—the quicker to anticipate the return.

A Final Look

Rod. I don't use the drop shot much myself, but it certainly has its place in the game. It's a good stroke to use—on clay—if you're behind in a match and want to break up your opponent's rhythm. Just make sure you can hit it. It's a lot trickier than it looks, and like every other stroke, you have to spend time to develop it. Some of the European drop-shot wizards work on the shot for hours, and they'll hit their share during the warm-up as well. If you can hit it, fine, but don't make the mistake of using it too much. The disguise element is important to the success of the drop shot, and there's no way of surprising an opponent who's looking for the shot every time you hit the ball.

THE TOPSPIN LOB

Roy. The topspin lob is a long way from being your average basic stroke. Most of the players on the pro circuit hardly ever use it. And with good reason. It's not a percentage shot. You have to hit it almost perfectly for it to work. The racket face is just about vertical when you make contact. It's almost a trick shot.

Rod. Emmo makes it sound grim.

Roy. Well, it is when you have trouble with it.

Rod. But if you can handle the shot, it's a great weapon against strong net players. It's not like a regular lob. For one thing, it's hit with a lot more pace. It's over the net man's head before he realizes what's happening. And that's where the topspin comes in. If you're hitting the ball with pace, you need the topspin to force the ball down before it goes out. The topspin does something else, too. Once the ball bounces, it takes off, making it impossible for the net man to retrieve it.

Roy. Enough salesmanship! Everybody knows that Rod Laver just about invented the topspin lob, so let's let him tell us all how to hit it.

Rod. I'll try, but it won't be easy. I was never really conscious of a specific technique of hitting when I was first learning this shot. I just kept practicing it and practicing it until I got to the point where I felt confident enough to use it in a match. Even so, I'm not surprised when I mishit it. You have to be prepared for a lot of mishits with the stroke. Sometimes you may mishit so badly that the ball will sail over the fence. And that's fine for baseball, but in tennis all it does is hold up the game.

A second very important factor in the stroke is keeping the grip extra firm. We're back to that nutty angle between the racket face and the ball again. Unless you hit it just right, the racket has a tendency to spin in your hand. That's why missed topspin lobs have a habit of ending up over the fence.

Roy. I have a feeling we're losing readers at a fairly fast clip.

Rod. I never said the stroke was easy. And I don't really recommend it unless a player already has his other strokes mastered. In any case, you want to try and disguise the shot as much as you can. Part of the stroke's effectiveness lies in catching the net player by surprise. And you want to give it a full follow-through.

A couple of more points: Develop your forehand topspin lob before you try to work off your backhand side. Don't worry about footwork too much, and don't try to hit it off every ball. Balls that come in very fast and very low are next to impossible to hit topspin lobs off. The ideal shot is a medium-paced ball that bounces about waist high.

Roy. I'm beginning to feel sorry that I brought the whole subject up to begin with.

The Basics of the Topspin Lob

The topspin lob, when hit correctly, will whip over the head of the net man and drop sharply in the backcourt, bouncing away with a mean snap toward the fence. Hitting it well requires a good sense of timing and excellent racket control. It also requires a tremendous amount of practice. The basics:

1. Get Ready As You Would for Any Groundstroke

Like any lob, the effectiveness of the topspin lob lies largely in the disguise factor. Rod prepares for the stroke as if he were going to hit a groundstroke.

2. Step Across Your Body with Your Front Foot

In order to get the whippy motion required by the topspin lob, it helps to get your front foot across the body before you hit. Having started with the body side-on, Rod sets the stage for the uncoiling motion that spurs the characteristic whip of the stroke.

3. Contact the Ball with a Pronounced Upward Whip

You have to swing with power if a topspin lob is going to work. The key is to whip the racket up and over the ball—notice the vertical plane of the racket head—making contact in the center of the racket and "carrying" the ball there for an extra second or two. To do this Rod cocks his wrist during the backswing and uncocks it with a rolling action as he meets the ball.

4. Take a Full Follow-through

The follow-through on the topspin lob is up and forward. This is one stroke in which an "open" body stance on the follow-through is okay.

A Final Look

Rod. The best way to master the topspin lob is to work with either a very cooperative practice partner or a ball machine. If you're working with a ball machine, set it at a medium pace so that the ball bounces around the service line. Start out by working on the timing, stepping across with the front foot, and uncoiling the body to get that whip into the ball. Then concentrate on the cocking and uncocking of the wrist. The more confidence you get, the more you'll be able to come over the ball and the more topspin you'll generate. Try not to get discouraged. This is a tough shot. It took me years to master it, and unless you're prepared to work on it for a long time, you'll never be able to make use of it in a match.

HITTING ON THE RUN

Rod. Tennis would be a fairly simple game if you never had to move more than a step or two to hit every ball. You could take your good sweet time setting up, get the racket back nice and early and generate a really smooth, rhythmic swing.

Roy. You're talking about geriatric tennis.

Rod. I know. But competitive tennis is mostly a game of running, of getting to the ball in time to get off a reasonable stroke. That's the trouble with too many instructional manuals: They don't take this factor into consideration. They tell you how to hit the ball when it comes to you but not how to hit the ball you have to run halfway across the court to get to.

Roy. Which we'll do right now.

Rod. Not so fast. Before we talk about how to hit the ball on the run, we have to talk a little about running itself—at least as it applies to tennis. Emmo was the sprinter in his younger days, so he'll explain.

Roy. I'll talk about it, but I won't use the sprinter comparison. It's more what we were talking about in the first chapter. Not so much speed but balance. That's why, when you move on a tennis court, you don't want to take too big a stride. The bigger your stride, the more pressure you put on each foot every time it hits the ground, and the more difficult it is to control your balance. Look at professional football players. The really explosive football runners—guys like Mercury Morris—don't gallop like horses. They run with their feet always close to the ground, and with a medium stride. That's why they can change direction so quickly and smoothly without cutting down on their speed.

Rod. That's the easy part. The hard part is stopping and still keeping your balance.

Roy. It doesn't have to be. What you have to do—at least what I've always done—is to adjust your steps while you're running so that you can plant your front foot down just before you swing. You don't usually have the time, when you're running for a ball, to set up the way you would like to, but as long as you get your front foot planted so that you can lean into it when you swing, you should be able to control the stroke. Another thing. When you're running for a ball, run with the racket already back. Beginners who can move well have a tendency to get to the ball in time but to discover, once they get there, that the racket isn't ready. They've done all the hard work but have still botched the shot.

Rod. But the main thing on many balls you have to run for is to forget about technicalities. If you move quickly and with short steps and if you remember to get that front foot down just as you swing, and if you have your racket already back, you don't have to think about anything else. And the funny part is how much better you can hit a shot you're scrambling to get to than one for which you have all day to prepare.

CHAPTER
4

Thinking About the Game

It has come to this. You have learned to hit all the shots and to execute them perfectly. In practice. Comes a match, you fold. Experienced players tell you that it's all in your head, and you believe them. You consult your psychiatrist, who tells you you will never be able to hit a tennis ball well until you resolve your oedipal conflict, overcome your subconscious fear of impotency (or frigidity), and agree to pay him $5000 in advance for a year of intensive analysis. You decide against it. You then consult a local guru, who advises you to eat only brown rice and vegetables, throw away your instructional manuals, and take sustenance from the Bhagavad Gita. "You're trying too hard," he tells you. "You have to not try." You try not to try but it doesn't help. "You're trying not to try," the guru tells you, "and that's the same as trying to try." You respond by planting a time bomb in his ashram.

Rod. Regardless of how much ability you have, how much instruction you get, and how often you practice, if you can't get your mind to work together with your body when you play tennis, you're never going to get very far with this game, and probably aren't going to have a whole lot of fun at it, either. The mental side of tennis is far more important than most people think. It's the one factor that pulls everything else together.

Roy. That it is. It's the catalyst, the force that sets into motion a lot of other forces.

Rod. Too many people, when they talk about the mental aspects of tennis, particularly about strategy, forget that the mental and physical parts of this game go hand in hand, and that all the thinking in the world and all the strategy in the world aren't going to do you any good unless you can hit the ball over the net. But at the same time, if your mind isn't working for you, all the talent in the world isn't going to do you much good, either.

CONCENTRATING ON CONCENTRATION

Roy. Most of getting your mind to work for you in tennis comes down to one thing more than anything else: concentration. Once your concentration deserts you, nothing else works. You can compensate for other problems. If your timing is a little off you can cut down on your swing. If your serve isn't working, you can slow it up. If one stroke isn't working for you on a particular day, you can work around it: run around your backhand, for instance. But you can't make any of these adjustments unless you focus on them and keep your mind, above all, on the bloody ball. And it doesn't take much to set your concentration wandering. You're about to serve. It suddenly dawns on you that you forgot to make an important phone call. Or you hear a plane overhead and you start thinking about a trip you're taking next week or took last week. You see somebody on the sidelines who reminds you of an old boyfriend or girlfriend. Or maybe your arm starts to ache a little, or you start to get hungry, and instead of thinking about the ball you're thinking about a Big Mac, or you're thirsty and thinking about a beer. And once you start thinking about these things, of course, you're no longer thinking about tennis, and your game is going to suffer.

Rod. It happens at every level of the game—even in the pros. One of the best illustrations I can think of is Arthur Ashe. When Arthur is playing his best, he can beat just about anybody, as he showed when he beat Connnors at Wimbledon. But you never know with Arthur. He can be running through you, hitting aces by the bushel, knocking off winners on every shot, and suddenly it all turns sour. Arthur's problem is that he tends to get down on himself if he makes a couple of bad shots. He thinks about them too much and he loses confidence temporarily. This is what probably happened in the 1975 World Cup Match against Newcombe. He had Newk down one set, and he was holding his own serve comfortably in the second. Then, serving at 40–love, and 3–4, he blew a couple of easy forehand volleys and dropped his serve. When this happens to me, I just try to put the game out of my mind. It's over. Gone. I concentrate on breaking back. Arthur, though, tends to play a little hangdog for a couple of games, and in this match, it cost him. He didn't give Newcombe any sort of a battle in the final game of the second set, and he just about gave away the first game of the final set. He got his game back eventually, but by then it was too late.

Roy. Not that Arthur's the only professional who used to run into concentration problems. We all do, to some extent. Few players concentrate as well as Rosewall, but I've seen his game fall apart, too. There was that Nastase match in Tucson, in 1975, when Nastase walked off the court while Kenny was serving for the match. Nastase was protesting a call, said he didn't want to play any more. Nasty eventually came back, but whatever edge Kenny had, he lost. Nastase won the next three games and then knocked Kenny off easily in the third set. Kenny's game just collapsed. It was 90 percent mental.

Rod. I remember the match, and I know how Muscles must have felt. Of course, it's easy for us to sit on the sidelines and say, "Well, the guy's a professional and so he shouldn't let a guy like Nastase get to him," but when you yourself are going through one of these mental slumps on the court, it's difficult to change gears. You keep saying to yourself, "Why is this happening to me?" and there doesn't seem to be anything you can do to change it.

Roy. The trick, of course, is to prevent the thing from happening before it starts. It's not easy, but it can be done. What most club players don't realize is that concentration isn't something that comes naturally. You have to work at it the same way you have to work on your strokes and your stamina. Whenever I play a match, I start to concentrate on concentrating as soon as I walk out on the court. I try to put everything else out of my mind but the ball. I played a match in California once when a helicopter flew right over the stands. I *heard* it at first, but I never looked up, and it never took my mind off the game. I concentrate so fiercely I never even recognize people in the stands—even my best friends.

Rod. And all these years I thought you were nearsighted.

Roy. The way I hit the ball on some days, I wonder if I *am* nearsighted. But in competitive tennis—at any level—there's no way you can overconcentrate, especially when you're up against guys like Nastase or Ion Tiriac, or anybody who uses the strategy of trying to psych you out of points, one way or the other.

Rod. You run into players like that everywhere in tennis. They like to think of themselves as "gamesmen." They'll take a little extra time on an important serve, maybe bounce the ball a half-dozen or so times. Or they'll call time out just as you're ready to serve and pretend they've got something in their eye. Or they'll start questioning calls or maybe go out of their way, when you're changing sides, to tell you how well you're hitting a particular shot—anything to get

your mind a little muddled. This isn't the way I play the game, and it isn't the way most of the pros play the game—particularly the Australians. Our feeling has always been that if you can't beat the other player with your game, then you don't really deserve to win.

Roy. I feel like singing our national anthem. But I go along with what you say. Still, you have to be prepared to deal with it when other players go into their little acts. Rocket did a nice job of it against Connors in Las Vegas when Connors was jawing with the crowd.

Rod. I just ignored him, the same way I ignore Nastase whenever he acts up. You sim-

ply say to yourself, whatever his problem is, it doesn't concern me, and the only way it's going to concern me is if I get involved, which I don't intend to do. I try not to think too much on the court, anyway. I know pretty much ahead of time how I'm going to play the match, and I've played enough matches so that I pretty much know what to do when the match doesn't go the way I want it to go. So mostly I concentrate on getting my feet moving and on watching the ball. If it's my serve and the other player is arguing with the linesman, I'll turn my back and just bounce the ball. Sometimes I'm grateful for the rest.

Tips on Concentration

Concentration in tennis is easier said than done. The trick, if there is a trick, is to put everything out of your mind but the ball you're about to hit. Here are a few tips that might help you concentrate a little harder (and probably play a lot better).

1. Remind Yourself Constantly to Concentrate

It's easy to forget about concentrating in a match, so get into the habit of thinking about it. Start concentrating as soon as you get out on the court, and every once in a while hold a little meeting with yourself just to get your mind back in gear again.

2. Forget the Last Point

You've just blown an easy overhead at game point. So what? Fretting about it isn't going to help you win the next point. If anything it will probably cause you to lose it. Once a point is over, put it out of your mind and concentrate on winning the next point. Tennis matches are won by players who know how to play the game one point at a time.

3. Don't Get Involved with the Other Player's Problems

The minute you start thinking about the other player, you stop thinking about your own game. And this goes for linesmen or people on the sidelines or players in another court. Keep your own house in order. If the other player is putting on a show, don't feed the problem by reacting to it.

4. Focus on the Ball

It's difficult, if not impossible, to think of two things at once, so if you're concentrating on the ball (really concentrating!) you're not going to have time to think of too much else. If you find your concentration wavering, try watching the ball, the whole ball, and nothing but the ball for two or three points. Watch it as the other player retrieves it. Watch it as it gets thrown back to you. And if you hit it out, watch it until it stops rolling.

A Final Look

Roy. There's a fine line between concentrating hard enough to play well and concentrating so hard that you forget about enjoying yourself, and every player has to figure out where that line lies in relation to himself. A lot of it, of course, depends on what's at stake in a match. If you're playing some friendly doubles or mixed doubles, it generally isn't necessary to concentrate quite as hard as you would if you were playing in a tournament or playing what you might describe as "serious" tennis. Still, though, it's not going to help your game very much if, after every point, you're talking about work or school, or telling a joke. Start doing that and the game gets ragged and it's not fun anymore.

I think it's possible to keep your mind on tennis and still be relaxed enough to have a good time, but save the conversation for in between games. Then, when you're ready to start again, give yourself a moment or so to get your mind grooved on tennis again. *Remind* yourself to concentrate. That little bit of time you take to focus on the game is probably the key to concentration. Let yourself relax a little. Catch your breath. Do a couple of knee bends if you feel you have to get loose. Then start to think about what you're going to try and do on the next point or in the next game. That was always one of my most successful techniques for concentrating: not just telling myself to move quicker or to watch the ball more closely, but having some definite goal in mind, like serving the ball to a particular spot on the court, or returning the ball in a certain way.

And if there's one thing you *don't* want to concentrate on, it's the point you just lost. Don't completely ignore it. But only think about it long enough to figure what you might have done wrong. Then pretend it didn't happen.

TENNIS TACTICS

Rod. Tennis is a game in which you can win a point or lose a point on the same swing, and it is around this simple fact that nearly all the principles of tennis strategy revolve. On most shots, it's easier to lose the point by making an error than it is to win it by hitting an outright winner. That's why a strategic philosophy based on hitting for winners on every other shot is hardly ever successful in tennis. Even players like myself, or Connors—players known for an attacking style of play—play the game with an eye toward the percentages. Tennis is a game of pressure: keeping the pressure on the other player so that he'll make an error sooner or later, and keeping the pressure off yourself. Every time you make an unforced error, you take the pressure off the other player and put it on yourself.

Roy. Rocket speaks from experience. When he was much younger, he never thought much about strategy or percentage tennis. He just went out and hit the ball harder than anybody else and figured he could blow his opponents off the court. He did, too—at least for a while.

Rod. But then I turned pro and suddenly started coming up against guys like Rosewall, Hoad, and Gonzalez every day. Now my go-for-broke style of play wasn't paying off anymore. A lot of balls that had gone for winners when I was an amateur were now coming back over the net, and I was making more errors. The pressure wasn't working on the professional players the way it had on the amateurs. That first year on the pro circuit was a shocker. I'd just won the Grand Slam in

1962 and figured I could slug it out with anybody on the pro tour. Then Rosewall knocked me off six of my first eight matches with him, and Hoad beat me seven straight times. It began to dawn on me that if I were going to win in this company, I was going to have to change my game a little. Play a little smarter. With more patience. Keep the ball in play a little more. Let the other player make the errors.

Roy. Play percentage tennis, in other words.

Rod. Exactly. Of course, everybody has his own idea of what percentage tennis is and how it works, but the basic principle is simply this: You don't beat yourself with unnecessary errors. You hit offensive shots or defensive shots depending on the situation. If the other player is attacking, you don't try for a winner that you have very little chance of making; you get the ball over the net. You force him to make the winning shot.

It worked for me. I started playing a lot more patiently, and it paid off. Instead of going for winners on returns of serves, I began chipping the ball back more at an angle. Not all the time; I'd still go for winners, especially on second serves. But I realized that by hitting a reasonably safe return, like an angled chip, I was not giving the server an easy ball to volley, and I was often in a good position after his volley to go for a winner on the next shot.

I used the same strategy on passing shots. Instead of trying to blast the ball by the guy at the net, I began chipping more and hitting low angle shots. And lobbing more, too—to keep the other guy guessing. Again, the same principle. You avoid the error yourself, and you make it next to impossible for the player at the net to hit an offensive volley. Now he's got to hit a defensive shot just to get the ball back, and if I move quickly I'm in a much stronger position to hit a winner—assuming, of course, I can get the ball where I want it.

Then the serve. As an amateur, I relied mostly on power. I used to serve flat to the backhand on first serves, and use a twist on the second serve. Obviously, the first serve wasn't consistent enough and the second serve didn't twist enough, because I was losing my serve fairly regularly in those first matches with Hoad and Rosewall. So I did a couple of things. First of all, I began to take a little pace off the first serve. I worked on placing it better instead of trying to blow it by everybody. It's something Gonzalez did well. People always talked about the power in Pancho's serve, but what really made him tough was his ability to put the ball wherever he wanted it to go. He'd pull you wide to the forehand side on one serve, and then go wide to the backhand, and every once in a while drill one right at you. That last kind of serve was the one that gave me trouble. By the time I'd made up my mind whether to hit it forehand or backhand, it was too late. Finally, I forced myself to slow down a little in between serves. That's a tendency so many players have—to rush the serve. It's probably the main reason for double-faulting.

I even made a change in volleying. A small change. Instead of trying to put the ball away on every volley, I learned to be more patient. I began going for safer volleys that had depth instead of sharply angled volleys that were either winners or errors. That made a big difference. By keeping the ball in play with a strong but safe shot, I was keeping the pressure on the other player. And that's what percentage tennis boils down to: keeping the pressure off yourself and on the other player. Every time you make the error, you take pressure off the other player. Every time you miss a first serve, you put the pressure on yourself. The percentage shot in tennis is the shot that strikes that balance between the pressure you're putting on yourself to make a testing shot and the pressure you're putting on the other player to make a good return.

Roy. And what can the average player learn from Rocket's experience? Quite a lot. The key to tactical success in tennis is control. It's more important than pace. You keep the ball in play longer than your opponent and you're going to win. This doesn't mean just poking the ball over the net. Take a full stroke. Hit out. But don't hit any harder than you can manage. There's a very simple rule to follow:

If you can't hit the ball ten times in a row to the same general area on the court when you're swinging at a medium pace, you're not going to be able to control the stroke when you're swinging for the rafters. Attack when you've got the opportunity, but don't be guilty of overkill. Here are some principles on percentage tennis that might get you started on the right foot.

Playing Percentage Tennis

Percentage tennis is not a "system" but simply an approach to tennis that calls for a combination of defensive tennis and offensive tennis, depending on the situation. Here are some of the main considerations as they apply to the various strokes.

1. Groundstrokes

The net is six inches shorter in the middle than it is on either side, and this statistic explains why crosscourt baseline shots represent a safer strategy than down-the-line shots. Line drive shots that barely clear the net and land at about the service line may look impressive, but carry too much margin of error. Better a backhand or forehand drive that clears the net by a couple of feet and lands not far from the baseline.

2. The Volley

Percentage volleys are hit with direction and not pace. The chief cause of volley errors is overhitting. Learn to punch the ball to specific sections of the court and to use the pace of the ball you're hitting to supply the pace of your volley. You do this by meeting the ball early and with a firm wrist. Strive for depth on volleys and be alert to the possibilities of "wrong-footing" your opponent. This is a simple volleying strategy in which you aim your volley to the same corner from which your opponent has hit the return. Chances are, if your opponent has hit a ball from the corner, he'll be moving toward the center of the court. A volley hit to the same place will usually catch him moving the wrong way. Choose carefully, too, the shots you come to net behind, and don't short-circuit your efforts by botching approach shots.

3. The Serve

Again, the same principle: Think less about power and more about varying direction and spin. Being able to place your serve is better than being able to hit it hard without controlling direction. If you're not getting at least 75 percent of your first serves in, you're probably serving too hard. Direct most of your serves to your opponent's weaker side (usually the backhand), but don't overdo the strategy. Move the ball around: down the middle, wide to the forehand, directly at him. And even if you don't play a serve-and-volley game, follow the serve to the net once in a while for the surprise of it.

4. Return of Service

Forget about hitting winners off the first serve. You may get lucky once in a while, but most of the time you'll lose the point. If the server is charging the net, try to keep the return low. If he's staying back, play a safe crosscourt return that clears the net by a couple of feet and lands deep in the backcourt. If you're up against someone with a very strong serve, move back a couple of steps and simply focus on blocking the ball back. Change the strategy, though, on the second serve. Move up on it, and if it's a weak shot, don't be afraid to take the attack with it. One of the best ways of blunting the attack of a strong server is to attack his weaker second serve. This will put more pressure on him and probably induce him to ease up somewhat on the first serve. The key to hitting a strong shot off the weak second serve is to get the ball early and meet the bounce before it dips below the net.

5. The Lob

Don't be shy about using it if you're under pressure. Keep it high and to the backhand side. Even if your opponent manages to smash your first few lobs for winners, it's no reason to abandon the stroke. Sooner or later the percentages will catch up with him.

6. The Smash

Don't overhit. Don't overhit. Don't overhit.

A Final Look

Roy. The best way to judge how much of a percentage player you are is to think back, after you've played a match, on how many unforced errors you made. If you've made a lot, chances are you're trying to do a little too much with your strokes. The next time you go out, make up your mind to play it a little safer, to keep the ball in play more, to let the other player make the mistakes. On the other hand, don't play so cautiously that you never hit a clean winner yourself. There's an offensive side to percentage tennis as well. If you've got an opening, take advantage of it, particularly if you're ahead, say, 30–love. If the opening's not there, settle for keeping the ball in play. Sooner or later, the opening will present itself—unless you end the point too soon with an error. Above all, play within your own game. You know—or should know —what you can or can't do. The average player who makes the most of what he has will generally fare better than the more advanced player who is always stretching for heroics beyond his capacity.

THE WINNING EDGE

Rod. I'd be a liar if I said that winning didn't mean anything to me. So would Emmo; we're both competitive. And close as we are, whenever we play each other in a tournament, friendship gets put aside. Emmo was the player I had to beat at Forest Hills in 1962 to win the Grand Slam. He was trying his best to win partly because he wanted to win but partly because he knew that I couldn't take pride in winning unless I was sure he'd tried his hardest. That's the beauty of this game. You can be fighting tooth and nail in a match, every point a struggle. Then, when it's over, you're sitting down together having a beer, the best of friends again.

Roy. Sounds beautiful. Trouble is, it doesn't always work that way with some players. It does for me, though. And for most of us who developed in Australia. Our feeling, basically, is that you go out on the court with the idea of winning, play like the devil to win, and if you lose, well, you've lost. So what? Nobody can win all the time. You have your bad days, and you even have good days when the other player is a little better. Why cry in your beer about it? There's always another chance.

Rod. How you feel if you lose, of course, depends to a large degree on how well you played. Losing isn't bad at all if you feel you've played your best. But it's sometimes hard to accept if you've beaten yourself. In fact it's *always* hard to accept it if you've beaten yourself. That's what people mean when they say that in tennis you really have two opponents: the other player, and yourself. Most players have more trouble with themselves than they do with their opponents.

Roy. Especially if you've let your nerves get the best of you. There are so many players around today who have all the talent necessary to be champions but who simply can't do their best in big matches. The pressure's too much for them. And with club players it's the same way. In practice, they do fantastically well. When it's time for a match, their games just fall apart.

Rod. It's something we all have to deal with. I can't think of any player who doesn't get nervous at the start of a big match, and if I'm not at least a little nervous, I start to worry because it means I don't care that much about winning. If you concentrate on your game, though, the nervousness should disappear, although it doesn't always work that

way. When I played Emmo at Forest Hills in 1962, needing only that win to give me the Grand Slam, I was so nervous on one ball near the end of the match that I hit a volley straight down into the grass. I wasn't aware of anything at that moment, and if it hadn't been for the fact that I was serving and the serving motion for most pros is pretty much automatic, I wonder if I would have been able to stay in the match. Emmo helped out. He returned two serves long to give me the match.

Roy. Not intentionally, I assure you. But if I were going to lose to anybody, I'm glad it was to Rocket. If I remember, we did a bit of celebrating together when it was over, and I have the feeling that sometime that night, I was under the impression that I'd won instead of him.

Rod. What helped me in that situation is a playing philosophy I've always had, which is that I'm not going to think too much about the other player when I play a match. Sure, I'll make some changes strategically if I'm not winning, but I pretty much play *my* game no matter who I'm up against. I reckon I have enough to think about without worrying about the other player. If *he* beats me, fine. Well done. I just don't want to beat myself.

Roy. That's a point worth talking about more because it's one of the principles Hopman stressed over and over. I remember a Davis Cup match I once played against Jan-Erik Lundquist, in Sweden. It was the first match of the Challenge Round and obviously an important match, and there I was down, two sets to love. Lundquist was playing well, and I was having a little trouble with the court. It was a clay court, and it had rained, and I wasn't able to get to the net quickly enough behind my serve. Okay, here's a situation where someone might say to you, "You're down two sets, the other guy is playing well —you better change tactics, do something to upset the other player's rhythm." Only Hopman didn't give me that advice. "Just keep the pressure on," he kept saying. "You'll get back in the match. Play your game."

So I did. It helped that the court began to

dry out a little. I won the next two sets. But then, in the fifth set, Jan-Erik broke me early and had a 5–2 lead in the final set. Here again, you'd think that a coach might advise a change in tactics. Hop didn't. He just told me to keep the pressure on—to play the percentages but not to play too carefully. I can still remember his telling me that Jan-Erik looked as if he was getting a little tight. "You win your serve," Hop said, "and the pressure will be on him to serve out the match. Maybe he'll get nervous."

He did. At 5–3, he was serving with new balls, and he double-faulted the first point. I went on to break him, and then went on to win the match.

Rod. I like stories with happy endings.

Roy. Happy for me. But it all comes down to what Rod was saying before—about playing your own game, and not worrying too much about the other player. If I had started to analyze everything Jan-Erik was doing, it would have probably got me so knotted up I wouldn't have had a chance against him.

Rod. It's true. And that's where concentration comes in again. The minute you start thinking about something other than the ball, you run the risk of making errors, of beating yourself. And you don't even have to be behind. One year at Wimbledon, Premjit Lall had me down two sets to love in an early round, when his game simply fell apart. What happened? I think he started thinking about how close he was to an upset and he got tight.

Roy. Who can blame him? One thing everybody on the circuit knows very well is that Rod Laver is most dangerous when he's behind.

Rod. I concentrate a lot harder when I'm behind, and I actually play a lot looser than when I'm ahead. But so much of it is confidence. You win a few matches by coming from behind, and comes a match and you find yourself down a set, you're not panicked. You've been there before and the pressure doesn't get to you. Not long after the Connors match, I had a couple of nice wins in matches

where I was well back in the tie-breaker of the final set. Tanner had me once 5–1 in the 8-point tie-breaker, but I managed to come back and win. Cliff Richey had me four games to love in the third set of a three set match during the CBS classic. The main reason I won in both cases is that I didn't panic. I've been behind many times before and I've come back a lot of those times. Having done it before gives you confidence.

It can work the other way, too, though. You get into a pattern where you let matches get away from you, and you reach a point where you get ahead in a match and almost wait for it to happen again. That was part of Stan Smith's problem in 1974. He'd lost some tough matches that he probably should have won, and it seemed to hang with him as the year went on. He'd get a lead and the other player would start to catch up and the players would tell me that you could almost see it written on his face—the feeling of, "No, it's happening again."

Roy. That's suicide in tennis—or in any sport, for that matter. You always have to think positively. You simply don't think about losing. Most of all you don't *worry* about it. The minute you start worrying about losing, you get tight, and when you get tight, you can't play your best.

People talk a lot about getting "psyched up" for matches, but for most players, I think it's more important that you stay relaxed and loose. I remember a doubles match I played once with Fred Stolle against a couple of American players, Jim Osborne and Jerry Cromwell, who were in college at the time. We were playing in Southampton, England, and the courts were in miserable shape. Somehow we managed to win the first set. The score was something like 29–27. And the second set was 7–7 when it got too dark to play. The continuation of the match was scheduled for nine-thirty the next morning, but that evening the people at whose house Fred and I were staying were giving a little cocktail party. Cromwell and Osborne got to bed early, but Fred and I didn't crawl into bed until about three.

And we weren't feeling too well when we woke up, I can tell you. A good thing for us the house we were staying at had a pool—a quick dip in a swimming pool first thing in the morning could sober up a skunk. I don't know what time Cromwell and Osborne got up, but they were already on the court, practicing, when we arrived close to nine-thirty. I guess they'd been there about an hour. They asked if we wanted to warm up, and I looked at Fred and looked at the court and saw how chewed up it was and realized that we wouldn't be able to get a decent hit anyway, and so I said, "No, we're ready to play." Osborne was so shocked that we weren't going to warm up that he lost his serve, and we took the next game to win the match. I don't recommend omitting a warm-up as a winning technique, but in this situation, at least, it worked.

Rod. What it proves is that for every "rule" in tennis, there's an exception. Earlier we talked about the importance of being yourself when you go out to play a match. On concentrating on your own strokes, and on your own game. That's good advice, but only to a point, and only for certain players.

Roy. And *only* for certain situations. Frequently when you're losing a match, it's because your particular style of play is working perfectly into the hands of the other player. Let's say you're up against a player who's returning every one of your serves like a demon, so that every time you go to the net, you're getting passed. Now some players are stubborn. They'll serve and volley, and serve and volley, and continue to get passed, and end up losing the match. A smart player, though, won't make this mistake. If he's getting beat with one style of game, he'll try another—assuming, of course, he can play a different style.

Rod. Which, by the way, is the difference between the good players and the great players. There are a lot of very good players around who play only one style of tennis. They're either baseliners or attackers. But the great players can beat you in a lot of different ways, so that when one facet of their game isn't working, they can turn to something else.

Roy. A good example is Newcombe. A lot of people think of Newk purely in terms of his big serve, but I've watched him win when his serve wasn't working. He's a master at mixing up his game so that the other player is constantly off balance. It's a simple enough strategy to put into practice, and yet so few players, especially intermediates, do it.

Rod. Mixing up your game works best against power players, the players who thrive on pace. It's tougher against the retriever.

Roy. Much tougher. I've seen it happen dozens of times in club tennis. You get a power player, one with great strokes and good speed, and you put him up against another player who swings a little awkwardly, but manages to get every ball back. And nine out of ten times, it's the retriever who wins. More to the point, it's the power player who beats himself. The temptation when you're playing somebody who's just nudging every ball over the net without much pace is to overhit, to get impatient.

My advice to anybody who finds himself losing badly when he is up against one of these players is to give him a dose of his own medicine. If he's giving you garbage, give him garbage back. Throw up some high lobs that land in the corner. Let him try generating his own pace. Be patient. Wait until you've got a good ball to follow and work the corners on your approach shot. Then try to angle your volleys rather than hitting them too hard. It's not easy to do, of course, but this is the only way I can think of to beat a player like this. Either that, or slip some arsenic into his orange juice in between games.

Against a power player who's playing exceptionally well, there isn't a whole lot you can do. The most sensible approach is to try to blunt the power rather than overcome it. I remember a great match one year in the French Championships, when Fred Stolle beat Tony Roche. When Tony was younger, he did much better when you hit the ball at him hard than when he had some time to think about and set up the stroke. So what Fred did was to come to net behind lazy shots to Tony's backhand. Tony had all day to prepare, but he was missing the shots. Not only that, when Tony started to attack more and more, Fred slowed down the balls even more and messed up Tony's timing so much that some of the slow balls actually passed Tony at the net. Eventually, Tony got to a point where the slower-paced balls didn't give him that much trouble, but it certainly cost him that championship.

Rod. There's the idea of percentage tennis again. Both Tony and Fred admitted that they were a little "tight" before, but Fred, who was a little more experienced, knew how to deal with it a little better. He put the pressure on Tony to make the shots. That's one of Rosewall's favorite tactics. You know that if you play Kenny in an important match, he's going to throw up a lot of lobs early in the game. He's testing you. If you put them away, fine. All he's lost is the point. But if you miss, Kenny not only gets the point, he

gets the psychological edge as well. He starts you thinking, gets you worried.

Roy. I've seen it happen dozens of times, not only with Rosewall but with a lot of players. The year Rafael Osuna beat Frank Froehling at Forest Hills, he did it more with his head than with his strokes. Froehling was killing everyone in the tournament with his serve, but Osuna played it shrewder than everybody else. Instead of trying to muscle the ball back the way everyone else had been doing, Osuna started mixing up his returns. On one serve, he'd stand well back of the baseline and just lob the ball back very high. Then he'd stand up close and just chip it back. True, not every player can return this way, but Osuna knew how to do it and it worked like a bloody charm. I can still picture Frank hitting one of those first lobs right into the net. You knew right there that he was in deep trouble. He started double-faulting, missing easy volleys. Osuna had destroyed his rhythm and his confidence.

The Basics of Playing Winning Tennis

You should be able to enjoy tennis whether you win or lose, but for most people winning is more fun. Every successful player has his own formula for winning, but each winning

principle presupposes an ability to execute the shots and maintain stamina throughout a match. Rod and Roy offer the following suggestions:

1. Scout Your Opponent Beforehand

If you're meeting your opponent for the first time in a match that it's important for you to win, you should, if possible, try to get a look at him or her in action. What are this player's strengths? What are his weaknesses? Is he a baseline player or a net rusher? What does he usually do with his second serve? Is he patient or erratic? Is there a pattern to his passing shots? Coming up with answers to these questions will give you a strategic edge before the match begins. Whether or not you can take advantage of it depends, of course, on how well you play. One thing to be careful of when you're scouting a potential opponent though is to let yourself become neither discouraged if the player looks to be much better than you nor overconfident if the player looks much weaker than you. Concentrate on the specifics of the player's game and not on the overall impression of it.

2. Get Grooved Before You Start

You can't expect to play your best in a match unless you're thoroughly warmed up. The point of the warm-up is twofold: to loosen up your muscles and to get your strokes grooved. Try to hit every stroke in the warm-up. Concentrate at first on watching the ball come off the middle of the racket. Make sure your feet are moving well. Make your goal a nice relaxing flow in your swing.

3. Play Each Point One at a Time

Good concentration begins with thinking only about the point that's coming up. If you've hit the last ball into the stands, forget about it. If your opponent has hit a ball that rolled along the top of the net before it plopped down on your side, forget it. Remember, all you have to do to win a tennis match, regardless of how far behind you are, is to win each point as it comes.

4. Mix Your Game Up

Frequently you can be hitting the ball well and still be losing simply because the other player is hitting the ball a little better. The best strategy in this situation is to change gears. Move the ball around the court a little more. Change pace. Throw up a few lobs. Mix up your returns. The purpose of this strategy is to disrupt your opponent's rhythm. Chances are you've worked yourself into a predictable pattern and you're making it easy for the other player to anticipate your shots.

5. Work on the Other Player's Weaknesses

Although there is a danger in concentrating so much on your opponent's weaknesses that you change your own game too much, the strategy is still basically very sound. You can generally spot weaknesses during the warm-up. In particular, try to find out early how effective an overhead your opponent has. If your opponent doesn't move too quickly or doesn't appear to be in the best of shape, make him work harder for his points. Keep the ball in play longer and hit short from time to time.

6. Adjust to Playing Conditions

More often than not, playing conditions in tennis dictate strategy. You need more patience on slower court surfaces—clay, Har-tru, etc.—and should come to net more on faster surfaces. If it's windy, you have to play your lobs a little more carefully, and you should also lower the height of your service toss. Lobbing when there's a blinding sun overhead might not seem like a sporting gesture, but it's well within the rules, and if you don't do it to your opponent, he may well do it to you.

7. Stay Calm

Easy to say but often hard to do. The key to staying calm in tennis is focusing on the ball and nothing but the ball. Take enough time between points to catch your breath and get loose again. Control your temper. Getting angry rarely produces better tennis. It just makes it unpleasant for everybody else on the court.

8. Change a Losing Game

Here's another one of those rules that has

more than its share of exceptions. The trick here is to be able to objectively analyze, in between games, what's going wrong if you're getting beaten. Are you beating yourself with errors? If so, why? Are you rushing your shots too much? Taking your eye off the ball? Not moving to the ball quickly enough? Hitting the ball too hard? Or is it simply that your strategy isn't working? Are you getting passed at the net, or getting beaten with lobs? Is your opponent teeing off on your serves? If you can figure out just why you're getting beaten, you can frequently make productive adjustments. There's always the possibility, however, that the reason you're getting beaten is that your opponent is a much better player than you. Should this be the case, play loose: You have nothing to lose, anyway. Concentrate on hitting the ball as well as you can, and forget about winning or losing.

9. Don't Play Serve-and-Volley Unless You Have the Skills

If you can do it, fine. Being able to follow your serve to the net and to hit a good, deep first volley puts the returner under tremendous pressure, but it takes a good serve, quick feet, and a sound volley. Serve-and-volley tactics work best on fast surfaces. When you're serving, don't rely on power alone but mix pace, spin, and placement. When you're moving to the net, go quickly but with control. Your goal should be to get to the service line before your opponent hits the ball. Be prepared, if necessary, to move laterally if the return comes to either side. Finally, don't try to do too much on the first volley. Just angle it deep and close into the net for what should be an easy second volley.

10. Use Variety Against the Net-Rusher

The good serve-and-volley player thrives on pace. Don't give it to him. Instead of blasting his returns, try angled chips and mix in some lobs. Once in a while, follow your return to the net. Whatever you do, don't get into a pattern with your returns. The same principle applies to passing shots. There are productive ways of getting the ball by a player at the net other than steaming the ball past him. There's no law that says you have to pass him on the first return. Try a low, soft shot—a difficult shot to volley. Then move in and pass him on the second shot.

11. Strive for Depth from the Baseline Game

Steadiness and depth are the two chief ingredients to a successful baseline game. Keep your opponent moving, which is another way of saying don't hit the ball directly to him. Mix pace, and don't be bashful about tossing in an occasional lazy blooper, just to throw off his timing. Patience helps. Resist the temptation to go for winners unless the chance for error is small.

12. Get the Most out of Your Net Game

Your net game in singles will only be as good as the approach shots you hit before you go to net. Don't make the mistake of trying to come to net behind shots hit from your baseline. There usually isn't time to set up. Wait for a short ball and try to glide a slice approach down whichever line you happen to be near. Then move quickly and alertly to a point about 8 feet from the net, a foot or so to the side of the service line down which the ball has been hit. Be alert but don't be over-anxious. You have more time than you think, and you don't have to use much muscle to hit a winning volley. Watch the ball, not your opponent.

13. When Ahead, Don't Let Up

Jumping off to an early lead in a match often gives you a sense of false security—particularly when you're getting points because of your opponent's errors. The tendency among some players is to let up, and the consequence of this tendency, frequently, is that the opponent not only catches up but wins. Better players usually dig in when they're behind. Remember, it's better to win 6–love than lose 5–7.

14. Enjoy Yourself

What does enjoying yourself have to do

with winning? A lot. Playing for fun means that you're playing free and easy and, in most cases, produces a better caliber of tennis. Play hard. Play aggressively. Play shrewdly. But, above all, play for fun.

A Final Look

Rod. Forgetting for the moment the tips we've just given you, I don't believe in any formula, as such, for winning. People have asked me through the years if I can explain the success I've enjoyed at the game, and I've never been able to answer it completely. Part of it, I guess, was being born with a certain amount of ability, and a lot of it was taking the time—devoting a life, really—to the game. But much of it I think has had something to do with the way I approached the game. I've always played aggressive, attacking tennis, and there have been some

matches, certainly, where I might have fared better if I had played it a little more cautiously. But on the other hand, I don't think I would have won nearly the number of tournaments I did if I had played the game differently. My attitude for most of my career has been: I'm going to go out and play my kind of tennis the best way I know how, and if that isn't good enough, well, that's how it goes. Yes, I'll change tactics in a match, but not so drastically that I am ever playing a defensive type of game. But that's me. I've always played a looser, more relaxed, and sharper brand of tennis when I was attacking. Whenever I'd start to play cautiously—like I did in the beginning of my match with Connors in Las Vegas—I'd end up not playing as well. So it all comes back to what we said back in the first chapter—that after you've had all the instruction and read all the books and watched all the pros play, you still have to play the sort of tennis that feels right to you. Winning and losing are secondary.

GETTING THE MOST OUT OF LOSING

Roy. Now that we've told you how to win at tennis, we're going to talk about how to lose. This may sound like a joke, but it's not. In fact, knowing how to handle defeat is one of the ways you become a better player. I'll go even further. If you're the sort of player who *never* loses, it's hard for me to imagine that you'll ever get any better. We get players of this sort all the time at our Tennis Holidays. They're the best at their particular club, but when they enter one of our tournaments and come up against a pretty good player, they suddenly discover weaknesses they never knew existed.

Rod. Which, of course, is what losing does for you. It points up your weaknesses. And if you can discipline yourself to focus on those weaknesses instead of moaning about the fact that you got beaten, you'll profit from the loss.

Roy. Every successful player does it. And the funny thing is when you really think about the match you've just lost, and think about it in a cool, objective manner, you come up with little insights that may surprise you. I remember getting whipped one year at Wimbledon by the Indian player Ram Krishnan. I wasn't aware of it during the match, but I was rushing everything—particularly my serve—much more than usual. And I was making errors because of it. And the more errors I made, the more I rushed. After that match, some of my friends told me that they'd noticed me rushing and had tried their best to signal to me from the stands to slow down. Okay, I lost that match, but the memory of it always hung with me when I went out to play other matches. And even to this day, whenever I make a lot of errors in a match, the first thing I ask myself is whether or not I'm rushing.

Rod. This is easier said than done. That's why a coach can be so important in a match. We give Fred Stolle a lot of ribbing about his being the "coach" of the Australian team in the Aetna Cup, in Hartford, but Stolle does more than simply hand out the towels. When Ashe had Newcombe down a set in 1975, Fred noticed that Newcombe was tossing the ball a little further to the right than he nor-mally does. It's a little thing, but it made a big difference in Newk's serve, and a big dif-ference in the match. Yet, I don't think it's the sort of thing Newk could have figured out on his own. You get caught up in a match, and it's difficult to keep track of the little habits you might be slipping into.

Roy. But we're talking now about being your own coach—at least after the match is over. Here's a little checklist to go over in your mind each time you come off the court on the short end of the racket.

Figuring Out Why You Lost

Nobody wins everytime he or she steps out on a court, but if you can develop the knack of reviewing the way you played objectively and not just shrug the whole thing off to bad luck, you'll be one leg up on most other players. Here are some of the questions you might ask yourself and some of the possible answers.

1. Did You Beat Yourself with Unforced Errors?

Everybody has his share of days when everything goes wrong, and if this was your first such day in a long time, don't worry about it. Write it off as past history and leave it at that. On the other hand, if this was the second or third time in a row in which you made more than your normal share of errors, maybe it's time you started rethinking the basics of hitting the ball. Think about the fol-lowing:

• **Eye contact.** Are you watching the ball actually come off the strings?

• **Footwork.** Are you getting your feet into position soon enough? There is always the tendency, remember, to get lazy, and that's where trouble starts.

• **Moving to the ball.** Are you moving to the ball quickly enough?

• **Concentration.** Do you have other things on your mind besides tennis?

2. Were You Physically and Mentally Alert?

You can always tell whether you're more lethargic than usual—mainly because it's im-possible to do your best in this situation. Try and figure out why. Too much partying the night before? Not enough sleep? Or maybe you've been playing too much tennis. It hap-pens. Overdoing it can hurt your game as much as not playing enough. Again, if this was the first time you felt this way, don't worry about it, but if it's becoming a pattern, take off for a few days. Do some jogging or light calisthenics but don't think about ten-nis. Then, when you come back to the game, start out by just hitting the ball for a couple of sessions instead of playing games. Don't go out to play again until you really feel hungry for competition.

3. Were You Out of Position for a Lot of Shots?

Generally speaking, you should play pretty much *your* game regardless of whom you play, but this doesn't mean that you don't make certain adjustments. If you're playing on a slow surface, like clay, and you're losing

a lot of points at the net, it's clear that you're going to have to play a lot more patiently. Next time out against the same opponent and on the same surface, concentrate mainly on keeping your groundstrokes deep. This will prevent your opponent from hitting shots that will pull you out of position.

4. Were You Nervous and Tight?

Usually, when you're nervous and tight in a match, it's because you're worrying too much about winning and not enough about just enjoying yourself. This is a problem every tennis player at every level has to face up to, and it's not easy. The question you want to ask yourself, above all, is why winning was so important to you. If you ask yourself this question after the match, the chances are you'll realize that winning wasn't as important as you might have thought at the time. Now what you have to do is keep this in mind the next time you go out to play. It sounds simplistic, but it works!

5. Were You Trying to Play Over Your Head?

Think back to the shots on which you made your errors. Are they shots you normally make? The fact that you can occasionally hit a winner off a particular shot doesn't mean that you've mastered it. Maybe instead of trying for so many down-the-line passing shots, you'd be better off hitting more lobs. And what about those double faults? Were you trying to do too much with your first serve? Remember: a player who can get the most out of his own game will usually beat a better player who continually tries to play beyond himself.

6. Were You Playing Out of Your League?

This may be the case more frequently than you're willing to admit to yourself. True, you may have beaten yourself with a lot of unforced errors, but don't overlook the possibility that your opponent was simply a much better player: more consistent and more experienced. Don't be misled by a certain awkwardness in playing form. Even if a player doesn't *look* very good when he hits the ball, his ability to keep the ball in play and to exploit your weaknesses will usually be the telling factor in your matches. Getting beaten in these circumstances should encourage you to practice more and, in future matches, should give you a standard by which to measure your progress.

A FINAL LOOK

Roy. It's easy to be a graceful winner, but not so easy to be a graceful loser. If you're the sort of player who hates to lose, don't torture yourself by thinking about the match before you've had a chance to shower and cool off. Give yourself some time. Later that day or even the next morning you'll still be able to run through the match in your mind and come up with some valuable explanations as to why you got beat. Don't be too hard on yourself but, on the other hand, don't deprive the other player of credit. "Luck" is a factor in all sports, but it's not as important in tennis as some people might like to think. There's always a reason for losing. The quicker you can understand these reasons and correct the things that underlie these reasons, the sooner you'll become a winner.

THE STRATEGY OF DOUBLES

Rod. People are forever asking how we became doubles partners, so maybe we should explain.

Roy. There isn't much to explain. It was obvious after Rocket won the Grand Slam in 1969 that he was washed up, so a bunch of us—

Fred Stolle, Newcombe, Rosewall, Roche—got together and drew straws to see who would get stuck with him. I cheated. I knew which straw was the shortest and I deliberately picked it. It was sympathy. I wasn't sure how the other guys would treat Rocket after he kept losing match after match for the team, and so I did it as a favor to Mary.

Rod. Emmo has great imagination. The truth of course, is that Emmo had begged about ninety different pros on the tour to be his partner, and everyone had managed to come up with an excuse. Emmo was getting so desperate he was willing to give away his share of the prize money, except that a lot of players figured that with Emmo as their part-

ner there wouldn't be any prize money. He was so depressed about it, he actually paid for the beer one night. That's when I knew he was in deep psychological trouble. And that's when I agreed to take him on as a partner.

Roy. It hasn't been all that bad, has it?

Rod. Not at all. We've had our share of success. We've got more than a dozen doubles championships under our belts.

Roy. The French Championships in 1961. The Australian Championships in 1969. The United States Pro Championship in 1971.

Rod. And don't forget Wimbledon in 1971. That was an especially nice tournament to win. It was the first Wimbledon doubles I'd ever won. It also helped me forget about losing to Tom Gorman in the singles quarterfinals.

Roy. And it wasn't an easy win by any means. Five sets with Arthur Ashe and Dennis Ralston. Rocket hit a beautiful shot to win it.

Rod. A forehand right down the middle, with Ashe serving at 30–40, 4–5. A great place to hit the ball in doubles. But 1971 was a good year all round.

Roy. For Rod Laver, certainly, winning thirteen straight matches in the 1971 Tennis Champions Classic to the tune of $160,000. Everybody said I had a good shot at winning one of those matches because I knew Rocket's game so well. Maybe too well. I lost in straight sets.

Rod. But that's singles. There's a big difference between singles and doubles—a difference that many players don't always recognize.

Roy. The obvious difference is that you don't have to do the work all on your own. You have a partner. And the better you work with him, the better your chance of winning. That sounds like an obvious statement, but you'd be surprised at how many very good players play doubles as if they were playing singles.

Rod. Not the best doubles players, though.

Roy. Not at all. You take a look at the best teams in professional tennis, and right at the top is Frew McMillan and Bob Hewitt. Neither one of these players has won a lot of singles titles, but they're a real good doubles team. It's a case of their working together very well as a team. Frew is a good control player who places the ball well. And Bob is a good, consistent, and heady volleyer with a great return of service who takes advantage of Frew's control by anticipating a lot of returns. Newcombe and Roche are a great doubles team. Newk is always tough on important points and has that punishing serve, and Tony is a solid, consistent volleyer—particularly off the backhand side.

Rod. That backhand volley is a key stroke in doubles. If you can be aggressive with it,

especially the way Emmo is, people will stand in line to be your partner. I think most of our opponents were much more concerned about Emmo's backhand volley than about my serve. In fact, Emmo's aggressiveness at the net was probably the biggest reason he won as many doubles tournaments as he did, and with so many different partners. Bob Lutz is another good doubles player with a fine backhand volley. It's one of the reasons he and Smith are such a good doubles team.

Roy. But what about some of the great Australian doubles teams of the past? Like John Bromwich and Adrian Quist. Or Ken McGregor and Frank Sedgman.

Rod. Both were super. Bromwich and Quist worked well together because both were steady and both were shrewd. McGregor and Sedgman were just overpowering—great athletes who played constantly aggressive tennis.

Roy. And combined it with a good understanding of position.

Rod. Position is really what doubles is all about. Power and speed are important in singles, but not quite as important in doubles. That's why a couple of cagey oldtimers can often whip a couple of flashy youngsters. The youngsters may have the power and speed, but the older guys appreciate position and consistency. And that's what wins.

Roy. Position, consistency, and something else: getting along well with your partner.

Rod. Yes. That may even be more important. I'm sure it's helped our own doubles game that we're good friends off the court. We accept the fact that each of us is going to have his good days and bad days. We don't criticize each other.

Roy. It's not always easy. There you are working your rear off trying to stay in the game, and your partner is missing sitters, double-faulting, hitting the ball out of the park. But it doesn't help to get sarcastic, or to get moody or angry. You're just going to make him much tighter. Anytime I've ever played with someone who's having an off-day, I keep telling him just to forget about it, to think about the next point. And it's amazing how many times the situation will reverse itself. My partner will start to play like hell, and I'll be making errors. Compensating for each other is also vital. I remember one doubles match Rod and I played when I had a sore back and I wasn't even sure I could finish the match. We won, though. Rod made a little adjustment when I was serving. And I let him take all the overheads.

Rod. It's a matter of not letting your ego get in the way. If Emmo and I are playing in a match and I've been having trouble with overheads, I let Emmo take them. If Emmo's not having a good serving day, I'll stand a

little further away from the net. Or maybe poach more, to keep the returner from teeing off. There are many different ways you can vary your doubles strategy to adjust to the situation. First, though, you have to develop a good understanding with your partner.

Roy. You've continually got to help your partner keep his confidence, even if he's missing shots. If your partner is having his problems, you're not helping matters by getting angry.

Rod. I like Emmo's style, but let's get more specific. Let's run down some of the key things to bear in mind when you're playing doubles.

The Basics of Doubles Strategy

Strategy assumes far more importance in doubles than it does in singles, which explains why cunning frequently triumphs over power, and why experience will often prevail over youth. A player with average skills in singles can be a super doubles player by understanding and putting into practice the strategic principles that differentiate it from singles.

1. Get the First Serve In

The cardinal rule of doubles is to get the first serve in. The presence of an opponent at the net puts added pressure on the player receiving service, but every time you miss the serve, you take that pressure off. Forget about aces. There are easier ways to win the point. When serving in doubles, stand about a foot or so inside the singles sideline. This will cut down the amount of open court your opponent has to aim for on the return. If you can manage it, try to come to net behind the serve, but if your serve—or volley—is weak, don't force the issue. Just make sure you're set for the return.

2. Keep Return of Service Low

Most tennis sages consider the return of service the most important shot in doubles. Among better players, the service return generally determines which side will win the point because it determines which side will command the net. The ideal service return in most cases is a low crosscourt shot. Not only is this shot difficult for the net man to poach (crossing over into his partner's half of the court to hit a return), but it's a hard shot for the server to volley as well. An occasional down-the-line shot is good preventive medicine against a poacher. On second serves, try to assume the offensive, moving in quickly, meeting the ball high and following the shot to net.

3. Take the Net Whenever Possible

From intermediate tennis up to the professional ranks, doubles is essentially a battle for the net position. Two players in tandem at the net stand a much better chance of winning the point than two players tandem at the baseline. The key to successful net play

in doubles (and in singles as well) is aggressiveness. As long as you're standing in front of the service line, you should never let a ball bounce. Hit your volleys early and try to meet the ball when it is well above the net. This will allow you to hit "down," forcing your opponents to hit defensive returns. Hitting "up" gives them the offensive initiative. Except for angled shots that are meant to be putaways, aim your volleys so that they bounce beyond the service line.

4. Lob Frequently

The crucial baseline stroke in doubles, believe it or not, is the lob. Since it's virtually impossible to pass two players at the net (it's certainly not a percentage shot), the only way to get the ball past them is to hit it over them. If you've hit a lob that looks as if it will get by the other team, your subsequent strategy should be to move to the net with your partner. On other baseline shots, the chief problem is keeping the ball away from the net man (assuming one player is back and one player is at the net). The general rule: When you're not lobbing, keep the ball as low over the net as you can without risking errors. Remember, the higher the ball, the easier the volley.

5. Work the Angles

In competitive doubles, the team that can consistently pull the other team out of position will generally win the point. Sharply angled shots, when hit successfully, will draw your opponents well out of position, leaving large areas of the court open. These shots needn't be hit too hard since the object is not to win the point on these particular shots but to open up the court for a relatively easy winner on the next shot.

6. Aim Your Volleys Down

If at all possible, the volleys you hit in doubles should be moving *downward* as they cross the net. When a player at the net has hit a ball at chest height or higher (lobs notwithstanding), his chances of angling the

ball for a winner are much greater than balls hit at belt level or below. Hitting down on a volley is impossible, of course, once the ball you're hitting has dropped below the top of the net. This is why quickness and aggressiveness at the net are so essential to winning doubles. In doubles, even more than singles, volleys should be hit early and out in front.

7. Hit Down the Middle

Hitting the ball in the middle of the court is generally not a productive strategy in singles, but doubles is a different story. A shot hit down the middle, whether it's a volley or a baseline drive, carries with it not only the possibility that neither of your opponents will hit it (each figuring the other player will take it), but it cuts down on the open court angle available to the other team. A player hitting a ball from the center of the baseline while his two opponents are positioned at the net has almost no working angle for passing shots and can only lob.

8. Poach When You Can

Poaching is sound doubles strategy providing: one, you don't miss more poaches than you make; two, you somehow let your partner know ahead of time so that he can cover the side of the court you leave open; and three, you hit the poaching volley decisively enough to end the point. The chief strategic value of poaching is the added pressure it puts on the returner. Once you've established that you can—and will—poach, your opponents have to play a bit more cautiously, and this takes some of the pressure off your partner. Poaching requires good agility and good timing. Try to time your move with the second the ball leaves your opponent's racket and have a general idea before you poach where you want to aim the volley. You should poach whenever possible, but don't overdo a good thing. Part of the effectiveness of this tactic is the surprise element.

The best way to combat a poacher is, first of all, not to let the poaching psych you out too much. Try to hit low crosscourt returns, but if the net man is getting to them, vary the strategy with a lob or an occasional down-the-line shot. Sometimes a return aimed directly at the net man is the best strategy, since the chances are he's going to be moving from that spot. Whatever you do, watch the ball and not the player at the net.

9. Move as a Team

This is an easy rule to remember. Whenever possible, you and your partner should move in tandem. If your partner retreats for a lob, you go back with him. If he follows his shot to the net and you're back at the baseline, you should follow suit. Moving as a team is especially important when one of your opponents has been drawn well out of the court on a sharply angled shot. If your partner, for instance, has gone far to his left to return a shot, you should immediately move toward the center to cut down on the amount of open court left unguarded. The biggest mistake beginners make in doubles is to divide the court into two sectors: "Your area" and "my area." True, each player should be responsible for roughly half the court, but the dividing lines are continually changing, depending on the situation.

10. Work Together

Two average players who complement one another's games will generally beat two players who are individually better but who neither communicate nor work well together. A successful doubles relationship is based on a realistic—and understanding—appreciation for each player's strengths and weaknesses. If your partner has a stronger overhead than you, it makes sense to let him handle any lobs that fall where either one of you could possibly hit them. A player who poaches well can frequently protect and compensate for a partner who has a weak serve. Talk to one another throughout. Encourage each other, particularly if one of you is having an off day.

11. Make It More Fun

The longer you can keep the ball in play, the more fun doubles becomes. Intermediate players could probably enjoy much longer and more exciting rallies if each player could discipline himself to think more in terms of keeping the ball in play than in hitting winners. The reason accomplished players can frequently keep the ball in play so long in doubles isn't so much that they return better, but that they hit safer shots, and hence make fewer errors. The concept of keeping the ball in play applies, in particular, to mixed doubles, which is usually a far more social game than regular doubles.

12. Play to Win

In tournament play, where winning takes on more importance, the fundamental rule of doubles strategy is to work on the weaker player (assuming there is a weaker player). A frequently successful—though not necessarily gentlemanly or ladylike strategy—is to aim the ball directly to the weaker player, especially if he or she is playing close to the net. If winning is the goal, the way you set up is important. Generally, the stronger player should take the backhand side. In some situations, the Australian formation (see page 38) can put added pressure on the returner, forcing him to hit his return down the line instead of crosscourt.

A FINAL LOOK

Roy. The average tennis player is going to be playing doubles a lot more than he plays singles in his lifetime, which seems to me to be the best reason to develop an appreciation for this particular version of tennis. Unfortunately, beginners and early intermediates run into some problems with doubles because players don't have enough technical proficiency to keep the ball in play more than a couple of times. But once you get past this early stage, the game can be a lot more interesting, more challenging, and more fun than singles. I like it more right now because I can play doubles a heck of a lot longer on a hot day than I can play singles. The key to the game, to repeat an earlier point, is not to confuse it with singles. The fact that you've got

somebody on your side to cover half the court and that your opponents are in the same boat changes your whole approach. Those great topspin passing shots that win points for you in singles don't do you much good in doubles. It's a game of touch and finesse, and not power. Also, I can't emphasize enough the teamwork aspect of the game. Tennis etiquette is always important, but never more so than in doubles. It bothers me to see a doubles team—whether they know each other well or not—arguing with one another on the court. It bothers me to see one player making it very apparent, just by his expression, that he's not very happy with the way his partner is playing. You should try to put yourself in your partner's shoes as much as possible. Think about how you'd be feeling if you were having a bad day and what you'd expect from your partner.

As for mixed doubles, the only thing I can say is that if you're a woman don't be afraid of it and if you're a man, don't turn your nose down on it. For most people, mixed doubles is played just for fun. This doesn't mean that you can't get some good tennis out of it, but it does mean that you don't want to concern yourself so much about winning that you're going to ruin a friendship—or a marriage—over it. One of the nicest things about mixed doubles is that the relaxed nature of the game, if everyone has the right attitude, lets you play a lot looser than you would under normal circumstances. So you're not only having a few more laughs but you may well be playing better tennis, too, missing fewer shots, controlling the ball more. Think about it, and then try to have the same attitude when you play with your regular doubles crew.

CHAPTER

5

*Having Fun
While Getting Serious*

The symptoms tell the story, and much as you try to hide it from your-self, the truth intrudes: You are a tennis addict. You have passed beyond the stage at which the game was nothing more than a pleasant way to spend a couple of weekend hours and have now reached a point at which things that other people never think about—like getting a better backhand—assume cosmic importance. There is now a direct relationship between the mood you wake up with on Monday morning and the number of easy overheads you blew the day before. At work, when you should be thinking about next month's figures, you think about last week's local tournament, in which you hit four consecutive double faults in the decisive game. At home, the lawn is going to pot (not to mention your kids), but you don't notice it and would never dream of devoting time to it that might better be spent cultivating your tennis game. The world for you has become divided into two types of people: people who play tennis and people who don't. Well-meaning friends suggest a month in the mountains of Switzerland, for a "cure." You consider it, but give the idea up when you learn that there are no tennis courts in the mountains of Switzerland.

Rod. Once you make up your mind that tennis is going to be more than simply a means of exercise and relaxation—and we're not recommending that you do or don't make this decision—you have to reconcile yourself to the fact it's going to take a lot of work. The work can be a lot of fun, if you go at it the right way, but there has to be an underlying current of dedication and seriousness.

Roy. It's like the old joke about the young Australian tennis player in England trying to find his way to Wimbledon. He gets into a cab and asks the driver, "Hey, how do I get to Wimbledon?" And the cab driver answers, "Practice, mate. Practice."

Rod. The driver was right. There's no substitute for practice. That and physical conditioning should be your main considerations if you decide you really want to become good at this game. Since Emmo is the resident physical-fitness expert, he'll talk fitness. I'm going to talk about practice. Actually, I could talk about practice day and night if I had to. To me, it's half the joy of tennis. Some pro-

fessionals hate to practice, but I'm different: I love to get out on a court and hit balls. I never get bored with it. I can do it for hours on end. Hit enough balls for a long enough time and pretty soon the tennis ball comes over the net looking as big as a soccer ball, and you get the feeling that there's no way you can *not* hit the ball wherever or however hard you want to on the court. When I get in that kind of a groove, I like to hit over the ball more and more, getting more and more spin into the ball. That's how you start to build up your confidence.

Roy. I'm not as emotionally wrapped up with practice as Rocket, but I get the message and I agree. I should also add that there's no way anybody is going to get good at tennis unless he or she is willing to put in practice time on a regular basis. You can't very well expect to hit shots in an actual match when you haven't hit them time and again in practice. The whole point of intensive practice is to get to a stage in your tennis when you're not thinking about the mechanics of stroking during a match, only where you want to put the ball. But it takes thousands and thousands of hits before you're even close to this stage.

Rod. And practice is more than simple hitting balls. To get the most out of a practice session, you have to go out with specific goals—the more specific the better. You may want to concentrate in one practice session on getting the racket back earlier on your groundstrokes. Or you may want to focus on one particular shot: a backhand down the line, or a high backhand volley. During a practice session, if it's long enough, you have the time to concentrate on the mechanics, to get your footwork right, to get a "feel" for the stroke. You can experiment a little more with grips or with spin. The practice session is a tennis player's laboratory. It's where you mishit all those topspin lobs so that when the time to hit one in a match comes along, you hit it perfectly.

Mainly, though, practice is where you develop the instinctive feel for how hard you have to hit the ball from different parts of the court. Lots of intermediate players make errors on short balls they should be putting away, and the reason is they haven't developed the instinct for how hard they should swing. In a match they have to concentrate not only on where they're going to hit the ball but also on how much muscle to put into

the swing. The instinct I'm talking about is similar to the instinct most people develop when it comes to throwing. If I ask you to toss a ball against a tree, chances are you're not going to have to think about how hard you have to throw the ball to reach the tree. You pretty much know it already, so all you have to think about is aiming the ball. This should be the goal of the tennis player who wants to get very good at the game, to reach a stage where all he's thinking about on every shot is not how to hit but *where* to hit it.

Roy. It helps, of course, to have a cooperative partner, someone who's as anxious to practice as you. They're not all that easy to find. Most intermediate players don't want to practice; they want to play. Fine. But there are ways that you can incorporate the two. Mix practice with actual competition. Play one game in which the only way a player can win a point is at the net. Play another game with each player getting only one serve (that will cut down on double faults, believe me). And really go at each other. The reason I used to enjoy practice sessions with Harry Hopman so much is the chance it gave me to stretch some of the other players around a bit, really give them a workout. The two-on-one drills were the most fun: two of us at the net and one poor devil at the baseline who had to run down every ball. Pure joy—that is, when you were at the net.

Getting the Most Out of Practice

The only way to become an advanced tennis player is to develop technical efficiency in a variety of strokes. Competition alone won't do the job. You need the structure of practice sessions where you're working on specific strokes and specific elements of your strokes. To get the most out of a practice session here are some suggestions:

1. Work Hard

It's next to impossible to re-create in practice the same psychological conditions that prevail in match play, but you can certainly re-create the same physical conditions, and even more. Chase down balls in practice as if the finals at Wimbledon depended on it. Don't hit balls on two bounces. Hit out. Ex-

tend yourself. And don't let up if you get a little tired. It's those last five minutes or so, after you're convinced you can't hit another stroke, that tell the tale and do the most good. Gut it out in those extra few minutes and you'll generally find you're not as tired as you thought. Discovering this will make a major difference in your stamina in a match when fatigue sets in.

2. Practice Under Different Conditions

If you practice only in ideal situations, you'll have trouble coping when conditions are less than ideal. One reason intermediates have so much trouble with wind is that they usually don't practice if it's too windy. There

has to be a near-cyclone before most outdoor professional matches are postponed, and most local tournament promoters operate the same way.

3. Integrate Some Actual Point Playing

Practice drills are fine for developing and refining technique, but if you don't integrate some actual competitive pressure in the drills, you may wind up in that sorrowful category of players whose beautiful strokes fall apart in combat. A good workable routine for combining practice and play in, say, an hour, is to drill for a half hour, play games for twenty minutes, and then use the last ten minutes to practice again.

Practice Drills

There are literally hundreds of different types of practice drills that are useful and fun. The particular drill you choose should depend on how much time you have to prac-tice, how advanced you are, and what, specifically, you're working on to improve. Here are some guidelines:

1. Groundstroke Drill

Instead of standing in the center of the court along the baseline during your ground-stroke rally, change positions frequently. Hit forehand crosscourts for a while. Then move on to forehand down-the-line shots. Repeat the pattern with backhands. Work on approach shots. And don't forget the ground-strokes that land near the service line. The main reason so many intermediates hit long on these shots in a match is that they never get the short stroke grooved; in a typical match quite a number of balls land in this area, and good players know how to take the attack on them.

2. Volleying Drills

Volleying drills present a special problem. The way most people practice volleys is to work with one player at the net and another player at the baseline. The only problem with this system is that the netman is generally hitting the ball back to the center of the court each time—a bad habit to get into. For this reason, three- and even four-man drills tend to work better for volleyers than two-man drills. With four players drilling—two up and two back—the net players can hit angled volleys and still keep the ball in play enough times to get into a productive hitting rhythm.

3. The Two-Man Aussie Special

This particular drill is the one Rod and Roy use more than any other. It starts out with Rod in the net position on one side and Roy back at the baseline in the opposite corner. Rod's job is to hit his volleys beyond the serve line on Roy's side of the court. Roy,

in the meantime, will use passing shots, chips, and lobs. The job of the player in back is to keep the player at the net moving back and forth. The reason this drill is so good is that you're forced to hit backhand volleys, forehand volleys, high volleys, low volleys, and overheads, and you're moving with every shot. You do the drill from both sides, and the net player and back player alternate on a regular basis. If you don't do that, one of the players is likely to keel over from exhaustion.

4. Two-on-One Drill

This is one of the most sadistic drills in tennis, and it has a couple of variations. In variation one, two players station themselves near the net with the sole objective of making the player at the opposite baseline run his legs off for every ball. After a couple of minutes of this torture, everybody rotates, thus giving everyone a chance to get in his licks.

In variation two, sometimes called the Kamikaze drill, two players station themselves at the net with three or four balls in their hands and do their best, within reason, to decapitate a player who is standing at the net across from them. To give him a reasonable chance, only one ball is in play at a time. This is a fine drill for developing quick reflexes at the net. Just make sure your insurance is up to date.

5. Serve-and-Volley Drill

This is a two-player drill in which you begin as you would during a match. The difference is the player receiving service has at least six balls close at hand. The server follows his serve to net, regardless of whether it goes in or not. The receiver ignores the serve but bounces and hits one of the balls he holds as if it were a return. The server must volley this return and, in sequence, hit a forehand volley, a backhand volley, and a smash, each of which is fed him by the player at the other end who is hitting balls out of his hand.

6. Aggressive-Net-Play Drill

Here is a good drill for four players who want to play more aggressive doubles. One team starts in tandem at the net. The other team anchors itself at the opposite baseline. Play begins with the baseline team in control of the ball. Their goal is to hit the ball anywhere within the confines of the doubles court with any shot—a drive, lob, dink, etc. —and try to get it to bounce before either member of the other team can get his racket on it. The goal of the net team is, first of all, to prevent the ball from bouncing, and second, to win points in the normal way. The only time you can score a point in this game is when your team starts out at the net. The only way you surrender the net position is by failing to hit a good ball before it bounces. Should you hit a volley that lands out or a smash that goes into the net, you don't win the point, but neither do you surrender the net. You start the sequence again. The baseline team can move to the net, too, but they can only earn a point when they've started at the net. What's the point of all this madness? To hammer home the idea of being aggressive at the net, of getting to those short balls before they bounce. You can play up to as many points as you like.

7. Racket-Control Drill

You and your partner station yourselves in the alley, on opposite sides of the net but not far from each other. You hit the ball to one another—easy—on one bounce until you can keep the ball in play ten times consecutively. Then you step a little further away from each other and repeat the process. The ball must bounce in the alley in order to be counted. Eventually you want to be able to keep the ball in play in this manner ten consecutive times from the baseline. That is control.

8. Concentration Drill

You and your partner set yourselves up on opposite sides of the net but on the same side of the court. One player puts the ball in play by bouncing it and hitting a groundstroke. The player on the other side needn't hit a return if he doesn't choose to, in which case the first player starts again. The point is in play once the receiver hits the return, and from this point on you play out the point as you would in a regular match, except for one thing: you must keep the ball on the side of the court where your opponent is standing. You can come to net, lob, hit smashes, do anything you would do in a game. The scoring gets a little complicated. The only way you can score a point is if you start, and the only way you can start is to have won the previous point. You play to three points, but every time the person who leads loses a point, he deducts one from his winning score. Too confusing? Not really. Let's say you started and won the first two points. Now you're ahead by two. But now you lose a point. The score stays at two. Now your opponent wins and now your score goes down to one. If he wins the point again, the score is zero. And if he wins a third time in a row, then he has one. The point of this drill is to concentrate on winning points in succession and to help you practice controlling the direction of the ball.

A FINAL LOOK

Rod. When it comes to practice, the simplest advice makes the most sense. Work hard and enjoy it. It's not hard to do both. It begins with practicing with somebody you get on with pretty well. Then it boils down to attitude and approach. When you go out to a practice session, make up your mind in the beginning that you're going to give it *everything* you've got. Remember, it's just as easy to pick up *bad* habits when you practice as it is to develop *good* habits, and the easiest bad habit to get into is to let the ball bounce two or three times before you hit it, or else to not even try for balls you're not sure about getting. Do that enough times in practice, and without knowing it, you'll start doing it in matches.

Something else, too. Practice is as much mental as it is physical. That's why it's not good to spend *too* much time on any one stroke. Your mind wanders. You start getting a little bored. So keep it lively. Wherever you can, get a little competition going. A simple drill like seeing how long you can keep the ball in play, can take on a different meaning if the player who makes the first error more often has to pay for the beer or for a hamburger after. And don't get the idea, just be-

cause you're practicing, that you can blow off steam and have tantrums that you wouldn't normally have in a match. If you find yourself getting frustrated and angry, stop for a moment or two, go on to something else, and then, later on when you're a little more relaxed, go back to the stroke that was giving you problems.

GETTING INTO SHAPE
(And Staying There)

Roy. We've talked earlier about what fitness and conditioning mean to tennis, so let's get down to the business of enjoying the whole process of getting into shape. It was never much of a problem for me as a younger player. I ran track in high school, and so I pretty much grew up on running and calisthenics. When I got a little older, I discovered a few other things, and as a result on some mornings it was a little difficult to enjoy running and calisthenics.

But whenever I was getting ready for a tournament—especially a big tournament—I would get into a routine that was designed to get me in the toughest possible shape. The

years I won at Wimbledon, for instance. Most players used to get ready for Wimbledon by playing some of the smaller grass tournaments in England, but I never thought that was such a good idea. The conditions aren't all that ideal at these tournaments. It rains a lot, which means the grass is often slippery, so there is the chance of a sprained ankle, and you have to spend a lot of time sitting around. Even worse, the grass gets so chewed up you never get a true bounce, which makes it hard to develop any confidence.

What I did, instead of playing these tournaments, was to spend about two weeks working out indoors, on wood, at the Queen's club. Wood is even a little faster than grass, but it gives you a much truer bounce. Great for building up confidence. I'd go there with another player, we'd do two-man drills all morning, and then play five hard sets in the afternoon. When that was over, I would go back to the apartment where I was staying and run some laps. Jog some. Sprint some. When that was finished, I'd do some gut exercises and push-ups. Then I'd get a shower, a massage, go upstairs for some dinner, watch a little television, and go to bed. I'd do that every day for two weeks, and by the time I got to Wimbledon I was feeling so sharp and toughened up physically that I was positive I could win. That's the beauty of feeling really fit. You don't have to pick and choose the balls you're going to run after. You chase down everything and you know that you're not going to run out of gas in the fourth and fifth set.

Then there's Rocket. Rod is just like Rosewall. They're two of the oldest guys still playing the major tournaments and they're in better shape than most of the guys fifteen years younger. Lew Hoad once said that Rosewall was the only one of the Aussies who never had to train. That was because he was never out of shape.

Rod. That's what age does to you. The older you get, the more you have to worry about staying in shape. You get tired a little sooner and your concentration starts to go. My game, as I've always said, is in my legs. When I get to a point that I don't think I can move well on the court, that's when I'll hang up my sneakers.

Roy. And look for another racket, eh?

Rod. I'm going to be nice and forget Emmo ever said that.

Shaping Up for Tennis

Getting into shape for tennis means developing first of all, a resilient body and, second of all, stamina. The more serious you are about getting good at tennis, the more serious you should be about conditioning. If possible, make it part of your daily routine. Running. Calisthenics. Walking more instead of taxicabs and car rides. Once you launch your program, go easy on the exercises and activities designed solely to *build* muscles. Weight training, for instance. Some routines with weights—wrist curls, etc.—are good, but brute strength is not your goal in tennis. Suppleness is far more important. Here are some basic exercises you can work into a program of your own.

1. Touch Toes

A simple stretching exercise that can do wonders for your back. Start out with your feet comfortably spaced. Then bend over from the waist, very relaxed, and let your arms hang loosely. Finally, with the knees straight, gently bounce up and down, trying to touch the floor with your fingers. It may be difficult at first, but within a couple of weeks you may be able to touch the ground with the palms of your hands. Do this exercise daily—when you get up, and when you go to bed. Start with ten. Work up to twenty-five.

2. Sit-ups

The fonder you are of beer and other fattening foods, the harder you'll have to work on your sit-ups. Strong stomach muscles are as important to a serious tennis player as strong legs. (Don't forget all the bending and stretching you have to do throughout a match.) Do as many sit-ups at first as you can do without straining. Eventually, you should be able to do fifty without a blink of the eye.

3. Push-ups

Push-ups strengthen the arms, the shoulders, and the wrists. Try some on your fingers too. Having strong fingers, believe it or not, can put extra mustard into your serve.

4. Deep Kneebends

Kneebends are super for balance and for strengthening the legs. Keep on your toes.

Start out slow, and go easy if you have problem knees. Ultimately you'll want to quicken the pace.

5. Isometric Exercises

Isometric tension (moving muscles against an unmovable object) builds muscle tone. A couple of minutes a day at home or at work simulating the forehand and backhand in an isometric exercise can have surprising results. Don't overdo it. Press a few seconds, then relax. Press a few seconds, relax again. You can use a desk or a doorway or even the arm of an easy chair.

6. Jogging and Running

A steady diet of running increases your endurance and toughens up your legs. Do more, though, than simply jog a leisurely distance. Mix distance running with windsprints. If you can't get outdoors or to a gym, run in place, varying the pace and the height of the knees.

7. Advanced Exercises

The Aussies call them "hooly-doolies" (and some other names, too). They're tough exercises used extensively by the Australian Davis Cup team. Tread warily if you're not limber or in shape.

V-ups

This is a real belt-tightener, excellent for the gut muscles and the muscles of the lower back. The idea is to "close" the V.

Straddle Hops

Agility can be developed, and here's one of the exercises that can do it. You jump high with your legs spread and do your best to touch your toes with your fingers. If you can manage even a handful at first, you're doing well.

A FINAL LOOK

Roy. It may sound a little trite to say it, but it's still true: The more you put into tennis, the more you're going to get out of it. Some of these practice routines and exercises we've just described may seem like a bit of a chore to you, but you can make them a lot more interesting and a lot more fun by keeping track of your progress and setting up some competition with yourself. The beautiful part of all of this is if you do get into some kind of a regular exercise routine, you're going to feel 100 percent better—and that good physical feeling alone is going to make a difference in the way you approach tennis and in the way you play the game.